HOW THE LIGHT GETS IN

Mary McEvoy is one of Ireland's most-loved actresses, best known for her portrayal of Biddy in RTE's long-running weekly drama *Glenroe*. As well as continuing to act, Mary is a regular contributor to TV3's *Midday* show, and also to Newstalk radio. *How the Light Gets In* is her first book.

HOW THE LIGHT GETS IN

My Journey with Depression

Mary McEvoy

HACHETTE
BOOKS
IRELAND

First published in 2011 by Hachette Books Ireland

1

ISBN 978 1 444 72211 6

Typeset in Sabon by Hachette Books Ireland
Printed and bound in Great Britain by CPI Mackays, Chatham ME5 8TD

Hachette Books Ireland policy is to use papers that are natural, renewable and recyclable products and made from wood grown in sustainable forests. The logging and manufacturing processes are expected to conform to the environmental regulations of the country of origin.

Hachette Books Ireland
8 Castlecourt Centre
Castleknock
Dublin 15, Ireland
A division of Hachette UK Ltd
338 Euston Road
London NW1 3BH

www.hachette.ie

To Larry and Catherine McEvoy –
See you next time around.

Contents

Introduction

'Show me a sane man and I will cure him for you.'
Carl Jung

From this Moment on

FOR MOST OF MY ADULT LIFE, I HAVE SUFFERED FROM DEPRESSION. It was a long time, however, before I gave it that name. For years after I was first properly diagnosed, I searched for a cure. I hoped that someday I would live my life free of the underlying sadness and anxiety that came with my condition.

Throughout those years, I read a lot of self-help books about depression. Many of them have helped me with my condition, giving me coping mechanisms or new perspectives on its nature. But I've always felt they were missing something. I've never found a book that has told me that not only is it actually okay to be depressed, but that it's okay to stay depressed, i.e., to learn to live your best life with the disorder, rather than seeking an all-encompassing cure.

For those lucky enough to have never suffered from depression – and quite a few people haven't and never will, even though one in four of us do, or will at some stage in our lives – it can be easy to think that people who are down in the dumps can and should snap out of it. However, those of us suffering from chronic depression might spend our lives wishing we could just snap out of it, but wishing is as far as we can go. We may have good days, we may even have great days, but our depression is always there, underpinning our lives. No amount of psychotherapy, alternative approaches to living or medication is going to make it go away forever.

Books about depression tend to be high on the hope factor. Unfortunately, though, by its very nature, depression is devoid of hope. So I'm not convinced that hope, per se, is the best currency for depression sufferers. Living in hope doesn't necessarily get you to the places you want to go. Why? Because it's a passive state, one in which you rely on outside forces to bring about change in your life. Optimism is the term I prefer.

Optimism is a lot less wishy-washy than hope. Hope is about an imagined future, whereas optimism is saying, in the here and now: 'This is where I build the future.' You act optimistically rather than hoping passively.

There is a great Buddhist phrase, 'honin myo', which literally means 'from this moment on'. The notion it imparts is that you are creating your life from this moment on. The future doesn't actually exist and, when you think about it, neither does the past. All we have is the present. Now is the gift. From this moment on is where all our power is.

Which is all fine and dandy for Buddha and the gods, but how can an ordinary mortal live completely in the present? How do you create your life from this moment on?

Introduction

Over the years, I have been up and down like a fiddler's elbow, but I have always kept going. Bizarrely, although my depression hurls me into the future with acute anxiety about the terrible things that may lie in store, or pitches me into the past, worrying over what I said or did and how it affected someone, it has also taught me how to live in the now.

We live in an age obsessed with self-help. Never before have there been so many books on self-improvement, and we could be forgiven at times for thinking that, if we're not on an active course to enhanced self-betterment for the good of both ourselves and humanity at large, we are in some way failing in our duty as human beings. For me, this is epitomised by the self-betterment machine of the Oprah Winfrey empire. The Oprah philosophy of living your best life, on what always seems to be a radical, heroic scale, leaves me for one, feeling as if I'm beaten before I've begun.

For a person who suffers from depression, the simplest thing can seem impossible. In a world that is constantly reflected through its media – which, let's face it, is the dominant way most of us are fed messages about how we live – the notion that we must always be striving for more, for self-improvement, perfection even, is something that in truth has very little to do with living in the now. Living in the now is not about self-improvement, it is about accepting who you are, limitations and all, at this very moment. It's not about changing yourself, just accepting yourself. Cue sigh of relief.

In the course of managing my own condition, I formed

*'At sunrise, everything is luminous but not clear.
It is those we live with and love and should know
who elude us. You can love completely without
complete understanding.'*
Norman McClean

a philosophy for myself. It's called the 'least you can do' philosophy, and I want to share it with other people who suffer from depression.

I came up with it one morning when I was in the vice-grip of one of my panic attacks. I was in rehearsals for a play at the time and had to get to work, but I'd woken up in such a state of whirling anxiety that I couldn't open my eyes, much less get into the car and drive to the theatre.

Anything I managed to do, I had to achieve in stages. I sat up in bed. I got my feet to the floor and I stood up. Getting to the shower had to be broken up into bite-sized pieces, if I was going to do it at all. That morning, if I had set my goal as doing a great day's work, I would have stayed in bed. Once I had got myself into the shower, all manner of things seemed possible. I was able to get dressed. I gibbered a few prayers in front of my Buddhist altar. I made myself a cup of coffee. After that, I was together enough to get myself to the car and drive.

In breaking things down into the least I could do, I harnessed my power. I lived in each tiny moment as my day began.

Introduction

Now, I'm not suggesting for one moment that everyone on the planet should suddenly start making a meal out of the journey from the bed to the shower every morning – but if you are depressed and can't cope, it's a very helpful strategy.

To create your life from this moment on, you need to ask yourself: what can I do *in this moment*?

If it's only making a cup of tea, that's enough. It's forward motion, a step towards making the next step.

The title of this book, *How the Light Gets In*, is inspired by Leonard Cohen's song 'Anthem'. Even in your darkest moments, Cohen tells us, our wounds offer us the possibility of transformation into light.

This is a book about living with depression. It's not about defeating depression or holding it at bay. It's my personal story of how depression became part of my life, how I identified it and how I have lived my life with it, while having a career in the public eye. It's about how I still live with it and about how my journey to reach an understanding of it is an essential part of who I am.

I've set out this journey in themes, reflecting the most important aspects of my life: family, work, religion, success, love, loss, happiness, ageing, death and home. For a person living with depression, all these facets of life are underpinned by the condition. This book is about living with that darkness and learning to take one step at a time – via the 'least you can do' philosophy – to find how the light gets in.

I

Family

'The flower will lose its beauty,
All fountains their water
The sea its birds,
The forest its beasts,
The earth its harvest —
All these things will pass before
Anyone breaks the bonds of our love
And I cease caring for you in my heart.'
Matthew of Rievaulx, thirteenth-century France

The Boldest Child in the Universe

WHERE DO WE GET OUR SENSE OF VALUE? DO WE GET IT FROM our parents? Do we derive it from our circumstances? Do we give it to ourselves? In the process of writing this book, I've come to the understanding that much of who I am, and much of how I feel about myself, stems from a deeply held belief that the only valuable thing for me to do in life was to make my parents happy.

This was neither their fault, nor mine. It simply just was, and still is, because even though they are both gone from this world, I recognise that I am in many ways still trying to make them happy.

When I was little girl, I always seemed to be getting into trouble over one thing or another. I thought that I was the only bold child in the universe. A few months ago, I found myself feeling a sense of great relief when a therapist I was seeing told me that I wasn't a bad child because I was wild and hard to discipline, and that many children are awkward customers. She recounted stories of her own son's eccentricities and her efforts to understand them. Even now, with all she understood about the human psyche, she had to dig deep. She told me of a passage she had read in a book on child psychology which suggested that instead of labelling children such as her son or indeed my younger self as 'difficult', that 'spirited' was a far more accurate term. We spirited children are difficult to deal with, that is certain, but we are not innately difficult. This word 'spirited' helped me to begin to accept the child I really had been, instead of being ashamed of the child I thought I had been.

So, I was a spirited little thing, really. Always running about the farm with grazed knees, climbing gates and trees, getting into everything I possibly could, never staying still for long. My mother was regularly exasperated by my carry-on, God help her. I was obstinate to a fault, never complying with her wishes, and I was always loud, shouting at the top of my voice and doing things I wasn't supposed to be doing.

Like the time I tightrope-walked on the edge of the manger in the cowshed and fell in, bashing my face so hard that my teeth were blackened and my lips became so swollen, I had a 'trout pout' for two weeks. I was forever pushing the boundaries my mother had set up for me, which mainly revolved around my being a quiet little girl who didn't go around getting herself into trouble.

'I can't leave you alone for a minute,' Mum would say, and when she was really annoyed with me, say if I was talking during mass or refusing to go to bed, she would show it by becoming monosyllabic. She never hit me or shouted at me, she just withdrew.

Poor Mum. When I was born, she might have expected that I'd turn into a refined country girl, someone with a disposition and demeanour like her own. She couldn't have been farther from the mark.

Anyone living in our homeland of Delvin, County Westmeath, who remembers my mother, Catherine Morgan, – and many still do – will tell you she was very elegant. She was strikingly good-looking and she carried herself well. My Uncle Paddy, her youngest brother, used to say of her that she had eaten a poker for her breakfast, but the words everyone else used to describe Mum were 'a lady'.

When she met my father, Larry McEvoy, she was a district nurse in Delvin. She had undergone her training during the Second World War and had worked in Manchester during the Blitz. My father had been an extremely settled bachelor of 55 and from a very solid farming background, well respected throughout the area. She was in her late thirties. I always have this romantic idea of my father spotting her in the village, and being captivated by her arresting beauty as she passed him on

'Call it a clan, call it a network, call it a tribe,
call it a family. Whatever you call it,
whoever you are, you need one.'
Jane Howard

the street in her well-fitted nurse's coat. When they eventually met at a gathering in somebody's house, I'd say she swept him off his feet. She must have, because within six months District Nurse Morgan became Mrs McEvoy, a farmer's wife. Nine months later, after the appropriate interval, I came along.

The fact that I was an only child is probably *the* defining factor of my life, the cause of much of my inner conflict. I think my mother had three miscarriages after me, but I'm not sure how I came by this information. Certainly, she never mentioned a word about them to me. Miscarriages were never talked about in those days by any woman, much less my mother, who was an extremely private person.

Possibly because I have no brothers or sisters to corroborate them, my early childhood memories are vague. I remember being in the cot in my parents' bedroom, looking at them through the pink wooden bars. I remember being moved into my own room, and being fine about it, even with the lights out. Mum and Dad weren't the kind of people who might say, 'Oh, do you remember when you were four or five, you did this or that?', so all I have to rely on are my own impressions and perceptions.

One night, when I was about five, I was saying my prayers and my mother said I should ask God for whatever it was that I really wanted. I put my hands together, closed my eyes tightly and said, 'Please, God, could I have a little brother or sister?' And then I stopped for a second before adding, 'And bring him tonight.'

True to who she was, Mum reacted in a very contained way. 'I don't think that's going to happen,' she said. Now when I think of what my mother was going through with her pregnancies, it must have been a very painful moment for her.

Despite my prayers for a sibling, I don't remember actually ever feeling lonely as a child. Because I lived on a farm, there was something going on all the time, and because of the men who worked for us, there were always people around, and lots of animals. I'd be out and about on the farm, making a nuisance of myself out in the hay shed, running here, there and everywhere from morning till night.

I had great pals in the neighbours' children and I'd go down and play with them. My cousins, who had lost their mother, would come and stay during the summer and we would have great fun altogether. I think my mother invited them in part because she wanted me to have the company of my peers.

My favourite early childhood game was running in and out under the bellies of our huge carthorses, like a little Jack Russell. How in God's name am I still alive?

I was a fearless child, with little sense of danger, but I will always remember the first time I ever became afraid. There was a programme on television called *The Adventures of Robin Hood*, starring an actor called Richard Greene. I loved the man with pure devotion. I think I was about five. In one episode there was a Viking ghost wearing a horned helmet and a cloak. I was so scared, I ran out of the room in terror, and had to be coaxed back in from the hall by one of my cousins. For years after that, I felt this lurking sense of menace around me. I became terrified of the dark and would always check under the bed before I got in, even in later life.

It is the first instance I can remember where I had an extreme reaction to a situation that, in some ways, would come to define me later in life. I think this is a unifying trait in many people who suffer from depression. We're very sensitive and we react. We're constantly internalising things that are, in fact, outside of ourselves. In our darkest times, we internalise the smallest negatives and make them huge. A sideways glance will become devastating to us; a tiny rejection takes over our whole being.

Although my parents loved me dearly, as I loved them, the messages I began to internalise from a very young age, whether they were real or not, were that my mother wanted me to be somebody other than who I was. She tried her utmost to get me to go to ballet lessons, but I was having none of it. Then she tried piano lessons: anything to give me a bit of girlish grace. In those early years, Dad was quite hands-off, like most fathers at the time, but I think he liked the fact that I was a tomboy. Mum, on the other hand, made it clear that she would prefer me to be a little girl in every sense of the word. And so with time, as I realised she wanted me to be different, I came to want to be anybody but myself.

Sabrina and Calamity Jane

WHEN I WAS SEVEN, I DISCOVERED AUDREY HEPBURN. THE film *Sabrina* was on television one day, and I was spellbound.

Sabrina is a film about a tomboy who is sent away to Paris and comes back as this beautiful woman in Givenchy dresses: an ethereal, waifish, ladylike thing, who now fitted in with the wealthy family into which she wanted to marry. The film had an enormous effect on me. Sabrina, or Audrey, was everything I wanted to be and was not. In my childish mind, I really believed that if I tried hard enough, I could be like her. My mother was probably relieved that I had such a ladylike role model, but, in truth, she was nearer to the real Audrey than I would be in a million years. Yet somehow Audrey became an identity that I latched on to in the search for one of my own.

I have held this fantasy about myself for a long time. I dream of my Cinderella moment – the transformation. The secretary who takes off her glasses and shakes her hair and everyone goes, 'Oh, but, Miss Jones, you're beautiful!' The girl who appears at the top of the stairs, and to whom everyone in the room turns to stare at in astonishment.

I wanted to be the ladylike girl who would never disappoint her mother. Who was stick-thin, who was glamorous, who spoke beautifully and who had an easy way with the world. Instead, I was a solidly built child, called 'Fatty Mac' at

National School by some of the kids. I have a mental image of myself walking in the schoolyard with a girl from my class, and I'm towering over her. Even though we were probably both relatively small things, I felt vast.

At the same time as adoring *Sabrina*, I also had a huge love for the film *Calamity Jane*, in which Doris Day played a rough-and-ready cowgirl with no social manners, who is at odds with everything around her. I loved Westerns and I was entranced by Calamity's buckskins; how she could ride and shoot as well as any of the men.

Halfway through the proceedings, Calamity gets her Cinderella moment, when her friend Katie shows her how to dress like a woman, in frocks and frills. I was disgusted when I saw this for the first time and proceeded to howl inconsolably. When she pulled a gun out from underneath her dress, I was mollified somewhat, but I was still seriously disappointed that Calamity had sold out to the frilly-dress brigade. I loved her power and I hated when, as I saw it, she chose to give it up, don the white wedding dress and, as the playwright William Congreve once put it, 'dwindle into a wife'.

Being so young, I thought that I could claim that power for myself, so I went around dressed as a cowgirl playing games where I made the decisions. As I got older, it slowly became clear to me that the self-determination I craved was only the stuff of fantasy. In reality, it was impossible for me to have any say over my destiny. I knew what I wanted but I didn't have the courage to fight for it. I remember crying many times because of the crippling difference between my fantasy and the real world.

My mother was determined to make a proper girl out of me, and a power struggle began between us. I wouldn't co-operate with the ballet or piano lessons and I deeply regret the frustration I must have caused my mother, who was trying so hard to broaden my horizons.

Yet, despite my resistance, I desperately wanted to transform from a tomboy into Sabrina, to be the perfect girl I felt my mother wanted me to be. At the same time, I wanted to stay just like Calamity Jane, a girl living life on her own terms without needing to change for anyone. As a female, everything I wanted to be and naturally felt I was – wild, unruly and questioning – was disapproved of by my mother. So I began to try my very hardest not to be who I was. That created a terrible inner tension, which was the cornerstone for the depression that would develop later.

With no brothers and sisters, all my parents' attention was focused on me. There wasn't somebody else being bold along with me. There was nobody to compare myself with. I thought that there was nobody in the world like me.

I remember an episode that, at the time, caused me to feel huge shame and embarrassment, innocent and all as it was. My mother had a friend who was quite genteel. She came for tea one afternoon and I got out all my dolls to show her, along with my teddy bear. I was always playing mother with

*'Other things may change us, but we start
and end with the family.'*
Anthony Brandt

my dolls, who had to eat their dinners and to go to the toilet and go to bed and all that.

I explained to this lady that my teddy bear couldn't go to the toilet because he had no hole. I wasn't trying to be vulgar, I was just being literal, as kids are. But mother could not hide her absolute mortification, and I squirmed with embarrassment as I retreated from the room as quickly as I could.

If I had had a brother or sister, we might have laughed about it, going, 'Janey Mack, you said "hole" in front of Mrs Posh Knickers!' but, instead, I internalised my shame for what I'd said. The episode seemed absolutely cataclysmic to me.

When I made my First Communion, my mother arranged for a photographer to come to the house. I had my hair in ringlets and everything was all set up, ready for his arrival. And then, just before I was to get into my dress, I asked my mother if could I go out and play for a while. She reluctantly agreed.

So off I went and hopped up on the little work pony that lived on the farm. For some reason, I decided that it would be a good idea to put a cushion on the pony instead of riding him bareback and the next thing my mother saw was me, flying through the yard on the pony at full tilt. The cushion flew off, and I came off with it. I don't know how I wasn't killed. I hit my head off the wall, got a big shiner on my eye and a badly sprained wrist for my troubles, just as the photographer was arriving at the house. My mother was appalled. She covered up the black and blue mark on my face with her make-up and bandaged my wrist. Then the photo was taken, with my head angled in such a way so the bruise couldn't be seen and my hand covered up by my white glove. The real Mary couldn't stop herself from being a humiliation to her mother and chastised herself for being such an embarrassment. The Mary in the photograph is her mother's perfect version of a daughter on her First Holy Communion.

And I can honestly say that echoes of this – of the sense of shame that rises up somewhere between my public and private self – remain even today. For instance, just recently, our local community organised a Halloween Fright Night at the community hall in Delvin, and I arrived dressed as a ghoul. I had a fantastic night, break dancing with the kids and getting up to all sorts of scary shenanigans, and the event was a great success. But as soon as I got home and into bed I started in on myself. I'd said the wrong thing to so and so, or accidentally insulted someone else. I'd made a holy show of myself dancing with the children.

To some extent, I'm still the little girl who came off the pony on the day of her Communion. I'm still chastising myself for letting go and being the real Mary, not the Mary in the photograph. For being Calamity Jane, not Sabrina. The difference is that now, I understand it. And understanding is illuminating.

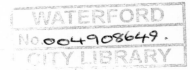

The Three of Us

ALTHOUGH CERTAIN NEGATIVE MEMORIES FROM MY CHILDHOOD stayed with me, as they do with any child, my overriding feeling is that this was a positive time in my life. I was loved dearly by both my parents.

There is a photograph on the dresser in my kitchen that I look at often. It's myself with my mum and dad, and in it I'm around six. We are sitting on a stone wall, me sandwiched between the two of them, squinting in the summer sun. To me, the remarkable thing about this photograph is our body language. Each of us is sat in exactly the same pose, our heads slightly inclined to the left. Even the position of our hands is identical.

We were a little unit. A team. It was Mary, Mum and Dad, all the way. I did not feel whole without them and, as parents, they were both solid as rocks in their different ways. They needed me too, in their own individual ways. And although in that photograph there is no physical affection on display – and my parents weren't ones for picking their little girl up and hugging her with abandon – the love between us was powerful. In fact, it was so powerful it could hardly be spoken of, as if somehow we had to contain it, rather than be overwhelmed by it.

So by any standards, I had a wonderful childhood. I have great memories of laughter. I have nothing but memories of fun, sun and joy in the summer days I spent with my cousins, who came to stay every summer.

Although it would be many years before I identified the condition I came to know as depression by name, I think I suffered my first real period of grief when I was 12, coinciding with the end of my childhood as I knew it.

My mother took the decision to send me away to boarding school. As I was a bit rough around the edges, I think she hoped it would smooth me out a bit. I know that she wanted me to get a good education so I could get on in life – and I'm sure she wanted me to be with other people my own age too.

My father was dead set against it. He desperately wanted me to stay at home. If he had had his way, I wouldn't even have been sent to secondary school, so desperate was he to keep me on the farm with him. My mother put her foot down, however. My bags were packed, my uniform bought and life as I knew it would never be the same again. I had never been away from home before.

I was sent to the Loreto in Navan, some 20 miles from home. To my mind, I might as well have been sent to another planet. From running freely around the farm, I suddenly found myself cut off from everything I loved, living in a strictly regimented place. Being in a dormitory full of other children was an awful shock for an only child – the lack of space, the lack of privacy. In the mornings when I got up, I would look out the window of the dorm and try to identify something familiar, any little landmark to remind me that home was near, that life was going on there as it had before I left.

Because I was the only one from a farming background, there was no other girl in the whole class with whom I could identify, no one to share my love of the farm or the freedom of running wild.

I would have to wait six weeks before I could go back to the farm again. I soon realised that six weeks is a very long time to a 12-year-old. I had never experienced anything like the aching loneliness of those weeks.

I would get up every morning at six o'clock and make my way down to the chapel to pray. I was often there before the nuns. There was another girl who was having an equally rough time and we would sit on opposite sides of the aisle, sobbing in unison as the sisters gathered for mass.

In my prayers, I constantly beseeched God not to let my parents die before my time at the Loreto was finished. This fear of my parents dying, which had begun with being sent away from them, was rooted in absolute love. I dreaded the pain and suffering I knew I would feel without them. When both my parents eventually did die, happily long after I'd left school, I had my own life, my own career, my own house, my own identity. Yet that dread of losing them was still just as intense. Every other relationship that I formed was second to the one I had with my parents.

Now, looking back on those morning prayers, I think I was praying to get back to the life I'd had before I left for school, hoping that nothing would prevent me being able to recreate my childhood with Mum and Dad on the farm.

But once you are taken out of somewhere, things are never the same again. Rhythms change, people change, and then when you come back, trying to fit in the way you did before is useless. You're different and no matter how desperately you or your family want you not to be, there's nothing you, or they, can do about it. The three of us would soon learn this hard lesson.

Home and Away

I NEVER SPOKE TO MY MOTHER ABOUT MY GRIEF AT BEING SENT away. If I had confided my unhappiness to her, I would have caused her unhappiness, and I wouldn't do that to her. What would the point have been? She couldn't go back and change anything.

And in so many ways, she did the right thing. Because Loreto Navan was quite a culturally driven school, I got the education that turned me into the person I am. It gave me an outlet for my artistic leanings, something that probably would never have happened back on the farm in Delvin.

I first returned home after six weeks at school, and after that on weekends and holidays. But nothing was the same. Gradually, my cousins were becoming teenagers and losing their interest in summer holidays on the farm. My contemporaries, with whom I had gone to National School, all went to the local secondary school and forged their own friendship circles, of which I was not a part. So my time at home was spent with my parents, who were a world away from the life I had at school.

Just before I went to boarding school that first year, I was taken to the dentist for a check-up. As I sat in the waiting room, I picked up a magazine. It was thick and glossy and I had never seen anything quite like it before. It was a copy of *Vogue*.

Isn't it strange that something so inconsequential as flicking through a magazine can be life-altering? There I sat, a plump, unremarkable pre-teen in a country dentist's office, gaping in wonder at page after page of gloriously beautiful, impossibly thin and glamorous women, who gazed languidly back at me. I was so entranced, I took the magazine.

This is it, I thought to myself. This is the world I want. If I can just be like this those women, I will be happy. Those haughty, urban models were strange role models for a tree-climbing, rural tomboy, who desperately wanted to stay at home living the farming life with her parents rather than go out into society.

During my first year, I felt like the odd-one-out at school, still Fatty Mac, never part of the loop. But, gradually, I began to make friends and became part of a group of girls who were also on the edge of school society. We were all mad about *Tara Telephone*, a publication that featured all the poetry young bloods of the day, which was smuggled into us by day pupils who sympathised with our bohemian leanings. We gathered in grave huddles to be 'deep', to talk about art, literature and philosophy. When we weren't philosophising, we were comparing weight loss, because second to our love of poetry was a growing interest in competitive dieting – we all wanted to look like Twiggy.

During my Inter Cert year, I started winning the diet competition. I remember going into a café in O'Connell Street in Dublin with Mum for a special treat, wearing a Kelly green miniskirt and a tight, black, ribbed top. I was fifteen and walking through the tables to get to the counter, I felt beautiful for the first time in my life. Like a *Vogue* model.

I weighed less than seven stone. At night when I was changing into my nightie, if I could see a bit of flesh in the dormitory mirror, I would decide not to eat the following day. Whenever we had a free period, myself and the gang would pore over cookery books, salivating as we took in every detail of the recipes. It was like our pornography.

During the summer holidays, my father would bring home apples for me. These were the only thing I really ate. One Saturday, he arrived with a box of apples, all individually wrapped. They were absolutely gorgeous and I munched down two in a row, after which I promptly fainted. When I came too, I heard Dad saying to Mum, 'Is she dead?' I opened my eyes and tried to stand up, but my legs gave way and I fainted again.

*'Just because somebody doesn't love you the way
you want them to, doesn't mean they don't love you
with everything they've got.'*
Anon.

I eventually came to and was able to stay lucid, but then I started throwing up the apples I'd gobbled down. I was put to bed and the doctor was called for.

When he came, he opened my pyjamas to feel my stomach and gasped out loud. 'You are like a something out of Bergen-Belsen,' he said. I think that's the first time my mother properly saw what had happened to my body as well. Apart from that day in the Kelly green miniskirt, I always wore my uniform, which was bulky and hid a multitude of sins.

The doctor gave me an injection and ordered me to start eating properly. The next day I went from literally starving myself to compulsively eating anything I could lay my hands on. I had built up such a fear of food that it was like the doctor's orders had given me a carte blanche to eat.

Mum never spoke to me about my weight loss. Although she ate normally, she always watched her weight too and if she put on weight, she wasn't happy at all.

A few months later, when I was beginning fifth year, one of the girls looked me up and down and said, 'You put it all back on.' And, with that, the dieting cycle began again.

When the Reverend Mother found out, my mother was

called and I was put on diet-watch. I was absolutely furious that the control was taken away from me. School life was regimented to a fault, and dieting was the only thing I had any say over. But the diet-watch was strictly enforced. All of us dieting girls were told what to eat and when to eat it, and we didn't get away with not eating it.

As well as an effort to change the way I looked, my dieting became an act of rebellion. Once, in my later teens, I said to my mother, 'If you see me eating too much, stop me.' Ironically, that started a very unhealthy pattern between us. She'd tell me I was eating too much and I'd rebel by eating more.

For all the rebellion, at the bottom of my dieting was the fact that I didn't want to be Fatty Mac anymore. Indeed, to this day, I have a horror of being Fatty Mac. Although I only suffered from extreme food issues in my teens – we didn't call it anorexia back then, but that is what it was – up until recently, I've have always been on diet. I've done them all, from weight watchers to hypnosis. I've been on every fad diet in the book and I've succeeded several times, but I always slip back.

If I had never gone on a diet, I believe that I would probably be naturally slim. For me, dieting was a process of deprivation and then, when the results came, throwing caution to the wind and eating too much again. My teenage dieting set in train a habit that was to last for decades of my life, but eventually I was able to find a way to overcome it.

Itchy Feet

AFTER I DID MY LEAVING CERT, I WENT HOME AND SPENT THE next 12 months on the farm. However, I had itchy feet, and I didn't pretend otherwise. My father, who was thrilled to have his daughter home for good at last, couldn't understand it. His little girl, who once loved nothing better than being with him in the fields, tending the sheep and livestock, wanted to leave again.

For my part, I only wanted to stretch my wings. Fundamentally, I believed my future was to manage the farm with my father, but, before I settled down to that, I wanted to explore some of the world that had been opened up to me through my experiences and friendships at school. I never intended my leaving to be permanent.

Dad just couldn't understand my need to get away, and while he didn't hinder my plans to leave, he certainly didn't hide his displeasure.

Again I was not living up to what my parents expected and, although I was determined to leave, another conflict that would lead to my later depression was put in place – my father's need to have me at home and my desire to fulfil that need.

Now that I am well into adulthood and am at last coming to terms with much of what made me who I am, I understand that the foundation of my depression lies in this deeply held belief that I could not be the child my parents wanted. Not that I blame them for wanting me to be a certain way. They had been brought up in an Ireland where you did what was expected of you and you didn't question it. You were obedient to everything – Church, school and parents. Authority was everywhere.

Mum and Dad just wanted me to fit in with the society into which I had been born, to do the 'normal' things everyone else did, because they believed that fitting in would make me happy. Looking back, it was as if I took each of their wishes for me and deliberately did the exact opposite.

My mother wanted an agreeable lady; I was an obstinate tomboy. My father wanted me right by his side, always; I left. One by one, I broke all the unspoken rules.

If I had sat down to my mother now and said, 'Mum, I'm going to be an actress. I'm changing my religion. I'm going to live with somebody I'm not married to. I'm going to be a blabbermouth on television. I'm going to go against everything you hold dear . . . Now, how do ya like them apples?' I'm not sure she would have been able to take it. Nonetheless, these were the paths I chose.

If I had sat down and told my father, 'Dad, I'm not ever really going to come home, even though you desperately want me to be here.' Well, I just couldn't have done that, even though it was the truth.

It was a catch-22. If I pleased my parents, I would be unhappy; if pleased myself, they would be unhappy. In the end I chose what I believed was the selfish option, my own path in life. But in doing so, I developed this belief: Being me makes my parents unhappy.

And as a result, although I fought hard for the right to make the choices I did, on some level they didn't seem like right or valuable choices to me. In some ways, they still don't. And it still saddens me, because although I know now that I have a right to be the person I am, it doesn't change the fact that I disappointed my parents.

As time went on, this belief extended beyond my family until it became: being me makes everyone unhappy. Ultimately it became: being me is the worst thing I can be.

When you believe that the very essence of you is bad, depression isn't likely. It's inevitable.

2

Work

*'When people go to work, they shouldn't have
to leave their hearts at home.'*
Betty Bender

Shine, and the World Shines With You

IT IS OFTEN THOUGHT THAT PEOPLE BECOME ACTORS BECAUSE they want to be noticed. And, indeed, we can be a flamboyant lot, but I have come to think that everyone wants to be on stage in some shape or form, at least metaphorically. Actors are just more honest about it. The person in the pub who talks louder than everyone else; the person who tells jokes constantly, whether you want to hear them or not; the person who seems to be in a constant state of indignation – they may not be on stage, but they all want to be noticed. We are all notice boxes. We all want to be seen.

Like many others, I have found myself being very disapproving of other notice boxes, probably because I saw myself in them, but lately, in my continuing attempts to think more kindly of myself, I have come to believe that looking for notice is an attempt at self-expression.

In my search to understand my need to be seen, I found a passage in a yoga magazine that really resonated with me. It described a young actor who told a very eminent yoga guru that he felt guilty because he'd always wanted to be special.

The guru replied that he *was* special, that *everyone* is special – that everyone is God.

I think that, in a fundamental way, in a knowing-in-our-bones way, we sense something deeper in our make-up than our personality, and we are subconsciously drawn to that deeper sense of identity. I have always sensed that, deep down in my being, there is a perfect energy that is not only the essence of me, but also part of everything else – universal perfection if you will.

This philosophising may seem a long way from the attention-seeking behaviour of the loud mouth in the pub or the joker telling his joke, but the truth is, we all have a yearning for acknowledgement, for proof that, in this challenging life, we count for something. We need to know that, even when we are alone and sometimes feel bereft and inadequate, there is a possibility that we are special.

Maybe our search for approval, our need to shine, is a craving for a place of rest, for a sense of ease with ourselves. Our ego tells us that we should look outside ourselves for that approval, so we look for attention. We seek to shine for others, rather than ourselves. We don't realise that rest and ease and luminosity are within us.

When actors mature and learn more about their own nature, they no longer want notice for themselves: they fight to tell the stories of the characters they embody by using their own experience of what it means to be human. They attempt to inhabit the soul of another, so to speak. They hold up a mirror to nature and, in doing so, often hold up a mirror to their audience. Their sincere portrayal of a character can give the audience a greater understanding of humanity.

Of course, they are seeking attention at the same time, but there's nothing wrong with that, is there?

Default Settings

THROUGHOUT MY CHILDHOOD AND TEENAGE YEARS, MY SOLE ambition was to manage the family farm when I grew up. I don't know how much of my wish to manage the farm was my father's ambition for me. Thoughts of becoming an actor certainly never occurred to me.

I remember seeing Katherine Hepburn playing Mary Queen of Scots when I was very young, maybe about six years of age. After that, I spent days wandering around the garden regally, with a tablecloth cloak around my shoulders and my head held high.

My cousins and I saw a production of *A Midsummer Night's Dream* on the television when I was eight. I absolutely loved it. For weeks afterwards, the game of choice was to wrap ourselves in ivy and play fairies in the garden. I was always the ringleader, and I was called Fairy Wickwire, a name and a role I created for myself (don't ask, I don't know either).

HOW THE LIGHT GETS IN

'The person who says it cannot be done
should not interrupt the person doing it.'
Chinese Proverb

I was one of those kids in National School who would be
offered a part in the sketches the class put on, so, obviously,
people thought I showed promise, but it wasn't until my later
years at boarding school that I got my first real experience of
the stage. For many actors, secondary school productions are
formative – they give an exciting taste of a possible future. For
me, they were the opposite.

Two productions stand out in my mind, both from fifth
year. The first was a pretend Gilbert and Sullivan operetta
called *The Geisha* in which I played the ship's mate. I had to
wear a pair of trousers for the part and I was hugely embarrassed
by the size of my backside in them, even though I'd kill for a
backside that size now.

A beautiful girl called Cecily, who had a sweet voice and a
lovely personality, played the coveted lead. I was a bit in awe
of her, with her amazing, winning qualities, none of which I
saw in myself. I was just the ship's mate with a big backside.
My big line came in the first half: 'I won't go to his party,
the brute!' It got a laugh every time, even in rehearsals. But I
didn't enjoy it because everything about the experience simply
highlighted how different I was compared with Cecily, the
personification of the girl I had always wanted to be. And to
cap it all, she had a lovely bum.

We had a new Reverend Mother at the time. She was a wonderful woman in terms of culture and education, but in terms of moral decorum, she was so buttoned up she'd make Jane Austen look like Amy Winehouse.

At 16, I was a very religious girl. I was absolutely devoted to Jesus and in search of a transcendental experience. At Christmas, I wrote a nativity play to express this devotion. I wanted to represent the real, religious magic of the birth of Christ in this play. It was to be a study in holiness and sanctity.

The trouble was, my devoutly religious play was being performed on the same night as a variety show staged by my class. My classmates wanted to put the nativity play on first and the variety show on afterwards, but I thought that the great holy transcendental message of my play would be absolutely lost, so I stood up to everybody and insisted that my play be the finale.

During rehearsals, one of the girls came up and screamed at me, saying, 'All you want is notice for yourself.' I was a bit freaked out by her, but I stood my ground and my play went ahead after the variety show, in which I was also scheduled to play some parts. We decided we would all wear our own clothes for the variety bit, instead of our uniforms. I had a white dress with a slightly low collar, which I thought was lovely. One of the other girls was wearing trousers and she didn't know her fly was open. We were having a brilliant time on stage, larking about, not noticing the rows of thin-lipped, stony-faced nuns in the front row. They were disgusted, so by the time my nativity play came on, all was lost.

I had named one the shepherds Voldi, after a character in the film *Ben Hur*. The girl who was playing Voldi's mother was from Cavan and she had a very strong accent. Every time she said Voldi's name, everybody thought she was saying 'Baldy', so in all my seriously moving scenes with the shepherds and the angel, the girls were falling around with laughter. Even I couldn't help cracking a smile. Baldy was a big comedy hit.

The angel I originally cast was an aptly ethereal girl, but she had caught the flu and had to be replaced by an angel who kept looking at her watch. I sat in the audience and watched my devotional play slide into giggling anarchy.

After it was all over, the Reverend Mother called us to her office and tore strips out of us for our shameful display in front of the nuns. To me, she hissed, 'You looked like a prostitute in your dress!'

I nearly died. All I could think of was what if my mother finds out that I was dressed like a prostitute?

I had caused trouble and was going to be an embarrassment to my parents. We were punished – I don't remember how – but it was bad enough that two girls ended up running away from the school, which was unheard of. And I felt somehow responsible for the whole sorry mess.

Although both experiences, mixed and all as they might have been, gave me a taste of the theatrical world, I came from a rural area where the notion that someone would become an actor was unheard of. I didn't know for many years afterwards that my father had actually been a much-admired amateur actor in his youth and had formed a drama group. The genes will out, and eventually, almost by accident, they did.

Accidents Will Happen

AFTER MY YEAR AT HOME, I KNEW IT WAS TIME FOR ME TO SPREAD my wings. I loved rock music and I wanted to go to gigs and see bands. At that time, you wouldn't find much of that in Westmeath, so I looked for a job in Dublin, mainly as a means to a social life.

The job I got was testing blood for brucellosis in cattle at the Department of Agriculture in Whitehall. There were lots of people like myself there, and many of them had the intention of doing something else more creative. Although it's hard to believe it of Whitehall now, the place where we worked was actually a farm at that time, with acres of green space. Sometimes, us girls would sit in the hay shed at lunchtime and have a great old time chatting and singing songs by The Incredible String Band. Our chat wasn't all about boyfriends or that kind of thing; we were very creative and talked about art and cultural matters. There was a touch of the maverick about so many of the people there.

I was bored in the evenings, so for the want of something to fill the time, I went to an evening class at the Brendan Smith School of Theatre on South Great George's Street. It was there that I met Martina Stanley, who now plays Dolores in *Fair City*. From the start, Martina wanted to be a professional actress. She was the first person I had ever met who had that ambition, or even thought it was possible. Slowly, knowing her began to open me to the possibility too.

I have happy memories of this time. Such as the summer's day when I went mitching from work and met up with Martina. It was a hot, hot summer, so I rang and told the supervisor that I had sunstroke and that I was feeling absolutely terrible. Martina and I went off and had a game of tennis in Trinity and then headed for Stephen's Green.

There was a band in the bandstand there, playing something from *Oklahoma*, and I started messing with my tennis racket, pretending it was a violin.

I got up the next morning to go to work, went in to pick up a paper and saw myself on the front of *The Irish Times*, full-face, pretending to play the fiddle with my tennis racket. An image of the picture of health chosen to depict a lovely summer's day in Stephen's Green. And there was I supposed to be polaxed with sunstroke.

When I returned to work, I was like a terrified little mouse. My hair was up in the photo, so I wore it down for weeks, trying to disguise myself. But if my supervisor saw it, she never said a word.

The Brendan Smith Academy was great fun. We put on little plays and sketches. I remember one sketch which had a Mexican girl in it so I put on my best Speedy Gonzales accent, which they all thought was hilarious. Then I ended up in a play in Trinity College. In those days, that's how it happened – you just fell from one thing into another. Somebody might see you at a club and ask if you would be up for doing something, so that's how I ended up doing this mime part in Trinity. I went down really well and it made me think that I had some potential.

Martina got a part on stage at the new Project Arts Centre in Temple Bar and her star began to rise. Suddenly, she was the young up-and-coming actress at the time, and that made me start to think that I could possibly act for a living. But in my mind, I was never that serious about it. If I got anywhere, it would be a temporary thing, until I went back home again to take over the farm.

I loved the acting world though; the whole bohemian way of it. Dublin was really boho in those days, with the Dandelion Market on Stephen's Green acting as a hub for hippies with musical ambitions and a whole crowd of creative theatrical heads clustered around the Project. We were all flying by the seats of our pants.

Then I got a part. A woman called Eileen Reynolds was directing a production of the Greek myth, *Antigone*, by the French playwright Anouilh, in The Project, and she wanted me to dance as the spirit of Antigone. It was my first proper professional job, a dance part no less. Stephen Brennan was the choreographer and the whole thing was very enjoyable.

It was a carefree, 'just do it' kind of life. I wasn't really taking it seriously, even though I wasn't doing anything else at the time. I had no worries about critics or success, or where the next gig was going to come from. And then one day, in the midst of it all, I decided I was going home. On the surface, like many of the big decisions in my life, it looked like I made it very quickly, but it was underpinned by guilt for being away from my father and the farm that had been with me from the moment I left home.

I had turned 21 and it was time to grow up. I was going to go back to Delvin to become what I was supposed to be. I thought I was going back to the Irish version of Walton's Mountain to play happy families. I couldn't have been more wrong.

Black Beauty

A FEW YEARS EARLIER, AT THE AGE OF 17 AND JUST OUT OF SCHOOL, I'd discovered a lump in my breast. Although I was completely freaked out, my mother was matter-of-fact about it. Having been a nurse, she didn't panic about these things too much. I was taken to the doctor and then into hospital, where they operated to remove the growth. Luckily, it was benign and there was nothing to worry about.

A year after returning home, the mortal fear of breast cancer I had felt when I was 17 resurfaced and I began obsessing beyond all reason about my health. I kept finding phantom lumps in my breasts, panicking that they were cancerous and going to the doctor every week to have them checked out. I was also developing other health issues to go along with it, like pains in my belly, which, in my fraught mind, *had* to be stomach cancer.

Two combined fears – that of mortality, and that of being mutilated – had joined forces and were waging war within me. It took a long time before I made the connection that it had all started with the decision I'd made to move home.

I'd taken it for granted that I would always move back to the farm, and never properly thought it through. Even though there was no outlet for my artistic side at home, the plan was always that I would return, and that was that. I had never formulated any real plan to be an actress and it didn't occur to me that I could change my mind. I didn't have enough sense of myself to say that I'd made the wrong decision, that, in fact, my life path was to diverge from expectations.

Dad really wanted me at home, but he didn't particularly want to give me the job as a farm manager. I was probably too young for it anyway, but nonetheless I had expected it when I returned home and so was desperately disappointed when it didn't turn out the way I expected. Still, I worked hard, looking after the sheep, grinding the oats for the meal, and doing all sorts of jobs on the farm. I'd be up at the crack of dawn, slogging the whole day through on my own. I was very lonely.

Although I hadn't identified depression as an issue yet, looking back now, I recognise that I was struggling with depression at the time. I remember watching the TV show, *Black Beauty*, on Sunday evenings. I would experience intense feelings as opening credits rolled, with the horse galloping through green pastures. I'd be moved by the horse's unfettered beauty. I wanted his beauty and freedom.

Although there was an undeniable, circumstantial aspect to my problems at the time, I have always seen my depression as having another, less tangible root. Often people prone to depression are missing what might be called a protective layer of skin which other non-depressive people have and which shields them from the negative forces of the outside world. There are some people who, through nature or nurture, have very strong centres and can stand their ground when the world is telling them to conform to something that's not right for them. I was not one of those people.

Over the years, I have done much searching into what gives rise to depression in a person. How does a child from a happy, loving background go on to become an adult who suffers from crippling self-loathing, or non-existent self-esteem? After much soul searching, it is my belief that some of us come into the world predisposed to it.

I am still very close to one of the cousins who came to

stay with us every summer, and we still spend a lot of time together. We come from the same kind of background and were brought up with the same values and methods. Yet she is the textbook example of relaxed self-acceptance, while I am often the hyperactive basket case. I see this when we go away on trips together. I watch her enviously as she goes through the day. She rests when she feels like it, eats when she feels like it, reads when she feels like it. She makes decisions and doesn't question herself constantly.

Meanwhile, I twitch with unease, always wanting the next thing to happen, always wanting to keep moving, while all the time having this co-existing, overwhelming desire to just rest. I honestly believe this essential difference between us arises, in part anyway, from our genes – we just came into the world that way.

It's not that depressed people are weak – they can, and do, endure a lot – but I must only speak for myself here. The lack of self-acceptance that I had felt from my earliest years and the desire to change myself in order to make myself more acceptable to the world I grew up in accelerated my journey downwards.

I always felt like an oddball at home. Now, coming back from bohemian Dublin where everyone had seemed to be on my wavelength, I was even more of an outsider.

There weren't many people my own age around, because all of them had gone off to jobs in Dublin or emigrated. And because I had gone to boarding school, I hadn't found friendship with people who would have gone to the local secondary school. I did putter around with a few people, but the harder I tried to fit in, the more at odds with everything and everyone I felt. I became very isolated. Whether I was truly isolated or not was another thing. Isolation can be a state of mind as much as a state of being – and what you feel when you are depressed does not always correspond to reality.

The creative part of myself, which I had been able to express so freely in Dublin, was now suppressed completely, and I think this was behind my obsessive-compulsive behaviour around the health of my breasts. But I could not see that at the time. I continued day in, day out with my farm work, doing whatever I needed to get done.

When the pains in my stomach came along, I was sure I was a goner. I was sent into a nursing home for tests. They found nothing, not even an ulcer and I was sent home with a clean bill of health.

Shortly after that, I actually discovered a real lump on my breast. I was taken in again and it was removed. It was lymphoma, but, again, it had been benign.

When I was in the hospital, I loved the banter of the nurses. There was fun and lightness there. Some of them were probably the same age as me and I felt more myself in their company. I could be fun and light too, joking around with them like they were my friends, not just people employed to take care of me. Their camaraderie and ease brought the bleak loneliness of my life on the farm into stark relief.

I didn't want to go home, but you can't stay in hospital for ever. Soon I was back working the farm, managing it day-to-day, but lost and shrivelling up inside.

In an effort to help myself, I joined an amateur dramatics group in Mullingar. They were a good bunch of people and they embraced me with open arms. We put on plays which would take ages to get to the point of staging, because we'd rehearse for an hour a couple of evenings a week and then it was off to the pub. Indeed, in later years, Mick Lally and I often mused together whether we went into theatre so we could go to the pub with a clear conscience.

It was on one of these outings to the pub that I met 'the musician'. From the beginning, I was very interested in him. He had long, brown hair, blue eyes and a louche elegance that stood out in Mullingar.

At last I had found someone I could be myself with: someone who talked about art and music, someone whose vision of the world extended beyond the narrow environs of County Westmeath, someone I could laugh with. Because he was my oasis of understanding in a world I couldn't fit into, I came to rely on him and I mistook my dependence for love. It was my first experience of thinking I was in love and, as many young people do, I mistakenly believed that if I was in love with him, he had to automatically love me back.

One day, six months into the relationship, I asked him if he did and he, being a man, hummed and hawed a bit. Outraged at his ambivalence, I stormed out of the house in a dramatic lover's rage.

HOW THE LIGHT GETS IN

'How lovely it is to do nothing,
and then rest afterwards.'
Proverb

It is hard to describe my devastation, but I remember it as if it was only yesterday. I felt as if a dam had burst inside me and I wasn't able to close it up again. I would wake up crying, spend my day working on the farm through a wall of tears, go to bed crying and wake up in the middle of the night having dreamt that he had come back. I'd go in to wake my mother because I couldn't stand the pain. For about three nights, she held my hand and comforted me, telling me there was plenty more fish in the sea, but after that she'd had enough. She was kind but absolutely firm. I had to get over this man and get on with my life. She was a practical countrywoman to her fingertips – throughout her life, that's the way she'd always had to be – and she could not understand the level of grief I was going through. Of course, looking back now, the loss of the relationship was the straw that broke the camel's back. Every dark feeling that was pent up inside had come tumbling out in an avalanche of distress.

Every time I went into Mullingar, I expected to see the musician coming around every corner. Every little thing, no matter how obscure, reminded me of him. I couldn't bear it. There was only one answer – I had to get away.

The New Girl in Town

IN 1981, RTÉ BEGAN SHOOTING AN EPIC DRAMA SERIES CALLED *The Year of the French* in various locations around the country, one of them being Westmeath. Our drama group was asked to be extras for a scene that was being shot in Mullingar Hospital. Inevitably drawn to the boho types, I soon started hanging around with people from the production. One day, I sat down with one of the crew and poured my heart out. 'What can I do?' I asked him. 'I need to get away and get some work, preferably in the theatrical world, but I don't have any qualifications.'

He told me that the Dublin Theatre Festival office was looking for runners, so I applied for a job there. The job, which I got, consisted of going around putting up posters for the festival, getting lunches for the people in the office and being a general dog's body. I didn't even think twice about leaving home, or the fact that my father wanted me to stay. I was so desperate to get out, I just packed my bags and ran without looking back.

I moved into a room in a friend's flat, and one of the people there told me about a new, professional acting school that was starting up at the Oscar Theatre in Ballsbridge. I decided this was my ticket to the future. Getting a place there would give me my big chance to move back to the city, and put me back in the theatrical fray.

My audition was on a Monday and as had become my habit, I went home for the weekend. I was a bundle of nerves while I helped out with the farm work, but didn't say anything. I will never forget my drive back up to Dublin for the auditions, in the worst winter weather conditions I've seen in Ireland to this day. I called my little car 'the deathtrap' because it was falling apart at the seams. All the way to Dublin, the snow cleared to the height of the windows on each side of the road as I rattled along.

I parked the deathtrap near the Bank of Ireland in Ballsbridge. In my mind's eye, I can still see the shoes I was wearing, bright red against the white snow as I walked along the street, steeling myself and thinking, 'I have to get in here. I have to get in here. I'm *going* to get in here.' Now that I had broken free, there was no way I was going back to the dark depths of despair I had experienced living at home.

I was so nervous that I cannot remember what audition piece I did. All I know is that, a few days later, I got a call to say I got a place at the school.

Going there was like being in a year-long episode of *The Kids from Fame*. All my anxieties melted away and I started having fun again.

Drama school was like being given a licence to make a complete fool out of yourself and not give a fiddler's. We were like a class of lunatics – all misfits, every one of us – and we became a comical little troupe, all supporting each other at the beginning of what seemed like a great adventure.

The Oscar School of Acting was run by a man called Chris O'Neill, who was also on the board of the Gate Theatre in Dublin. About six months into the course, he secured audition spots for our class for the Gate production of George Bernard Shaw's *The Philanderer*. I auditioned and ended up getting the part of Sylvia Craven, a precocious ingénue. She was a bit like the comedy character that I played in *The Geisha* back in school, except she was a girl and had a lot more lines.

All my classmates were screaming, roaring and jumping up and down with excitement when I got the part. I couldn't quite believe it myself. There I was, barely a few months from being down, depressed and sure my life would never consist of anything but farming and loneliness, rehearsing on the stage of The Gate alongside Barbara Brennan, Dermot Tuohy, Maria McDermottroe, Aiden Grenell and Christopher Casson – the crème de la crème of Ireland's theatrical elite.

I was like a puppy, lapping it all up and loving just about everything about it. Except for Dermot Touhy, who didn't like me very much. He thought I was way too giddy for my own good.

The director wanted me to braid my hair to give it an Edwardian look, but it didn't work because my hair was too short. So instead they decided to get me a wig. I wasn't best pleased about this, having always felt that, with my wide face, I best resemble a mushroom with one on!

Anyway, the dress rehearsal came, and I donned the dreaded

wig. In my naïveté, I didn't realise that if there was something about you on stage that was different, you had to tell the other actors beforehand, so as not to put them off. I entered stage left, looking like something out of the Jackson Five, and Dermot lost his lines, and his temper.

He was shouting, 'How can you expect to act with *that* in the wings?' and I was sent off with a flea in my ear.

The costume designer gave up the wig as a bad job and I was sent away to get my hair permed. Dermot grudgingly judged the perm an improvement and *The Philanderer* was a great success. Suddenly, I was the new girl in town.

Glenroe

IF YOU ARE CAST IN A PLAY IN A THEATRE AND THERE'S A SUITABLE part in the following production, you have a strong chance of getting it. And so I landed a part in Mary Halpin's *Semi-Private*, where I played a tea lady on a hospital ward. I was cutting my teeth, as they say, while keeping an eye out for the next thing.

By this time, I had acquired an agent, and word came through about auditions for a new television show on RTÉ, which was to replace *Bracken*, the rural drama that had spun off from *The Riordans*.

I did my audition for *Glenroe* with Mick Lally. I was

completely starstruck. I hadn't met Mick before, but I was a big fan of Dinny and Miley on *Bracken*, the characters played by Joe Lynch and Mick who were being transplanted into *Glenroe*.

The audition was the scene where Biddy talked to Miley for the first time. Mick was courteous and friendly, and I think I blushed the whole way through. Two days later, I got a phone call from my agent, who said they were offering the part to someone else. I was fine about it, because I didn't think I was in with a chance in the first place.

I had also gone up for a small part in the children's TV show *Wanderly Wagon* at the time, but hadn't heard anything back. I was at home in Delvin a few weeks later when I got a phone call from an RTÉ producer called Brían Maclochlainn.

'We're just calling to say you've got the part,' he said.

I assumed he was talking about *Wanderly Wagon*. 'That's grand, thanks,' I replied.

I think he was a bit taken aback by my casual tone. I asked him what the name of the character was.

'Biddy,' came the reply.

'What?'

'Biddy, the part you auditioned for in *Glenroe*.'

I nearly fell out of my standing. It turned out that they had offered Biddy to three other people and all of them either had other jobs or didn't want to get caught up in a television series. So they ended up picking me.

I remember one day at the very beginning, when I was shooting a scene in a car with Joe Lynch on a road in Wicklow, with a garda stopping traffic either way to give us space. I suddenly realised it was the anniversary of the day the musician had dumped me.

I thought, 'This time last year I was in the depths of a misery that I thought would never end and here I am now with Joe Lynch, in a television series, happier than I have ever been.' Life truly is amazing, the way it can change completely, sometimes in the blink of an eye.

And, just in case I should lose the run of myself, with that I promptly started the car and ran over the garda's shiny new motorbike. I hope RTÉ picked up the bill, because I certainly didn't!

I think RTÉ intended *Glenroe* to be a sort of stepping-stone between the ending of *Bracken* and a new urban series, which ultimately became *Fair City*. But everybody was surprised by how popular it was. It seemed like the whole country was watching it religiously from episode one.

Although *Glenroe* was my main source of income for 16 years, during which time I became inextricably linked with my character Biddy Byrne, I continued to work in the theatre throughout, during the yearly three-month break from filming.

When the very first episode of *Glenroe* was aired, I was in Galway, acting alongside Mick in a Druid production of M.J. Molloy's *The Wood of the Whispering*. An actor in the play and his wife made fresh pasta and bought tequila, and we all sat down and watched the show. I was so nervous, I drank too much tequila and ended up throwing up in the garden.

Most actors will tell you that they hate looking at themselves. Even the most beautiful and talented Hollywood stars say that. For me, as *Glenroe* went on, I found it harder to look at myself. I watched it the odd time. Sometimes a scene would work really well and I'd be happy with it and I'd want to see it, but other than that, I didn't like it because I'd only find things to criticise about my performance.

That first year, while we were touring around Ireland with *The Wood of the Whispering*, I kind of forgot all about *Glenroe*. Mick was recognised everywhere – he was the 'name' from the show, so he got all the attention. We played in ballrooms and community halls across the country and the play always went down a storm.

During the months we were filming *Glenroe*, I continued to go home to my parents and the farm every weekend. Daddy still wasn't very happy with me being away from home. I don't think Mum quite knew what to make of the acting thing. It wasn't something that was chosen for me, but if I was on television I must be good.

I became more torn as the years went on between the two things, acting and the farm. But at the beginning of *Glenroe*, I was in my late twenties. It was the 1980s and, unlike most of my peers, I had a steady and plentiful income. It was a relatively carefree time, and for the first time in a long time, I was having great fun.

My Other Family

WHEN I DECIDED TO BECOME AN ACTRESS, I WAS, IN A SENSE, given access to another kind of family, one that accepted me completely just for being me. There were lots of people in the profession who seemed to be just the same as I was – people who didn't go to mass, people who lived together instead of getting married, people interested in the arts. I hadn't completely shed the lifelong feeling that I was always the odd one out in a group, but here I wasn't as odd as I was in my other family.

For my 16 years working on *Glenroe*, I was lucky enough to become part of an incredibly close family unit away from my biological family. As families go, my *Glenroe* one was very functional. We all had our roles to play, both in front of and behind the camera and we all got on with it, without too much conflict. To this day, many of us remain firm friends.

When I was working, my life was extremely structured, and I found this very comforting. The controlled environment of television really appealed to me. In studio, I was cut off from the world, safely out of the way of harm, and I loved the noise the big soundproofed studio door made as it closed when we prepared to shoot a scene. For at least the next 20 minutes, I knew exactly what was required of me and I could do it very well.

I felt utterly at home in front of the camera, completely at my ease. It was like I was meant to do this – I was meant to be a television actor or a film actor. I had this coolness under pressure, which was interesting, considering how easily I get distracted by things in the 'real world'.

In between takes, laughter was a constant sound on the set. Often the girls would huddle together discussing our troubles, which could be anything from weight gain to serious illness, and just as we were getting bogged down, some of the boys would appear from nowhere and say or do something so ridiculously funny that all troubles would be forgotten as we fell about the place with tears of laughter rolling down our faces.

I remember going in one day and saying to one of the cast, 'You know something? These are the good old days.'

I wanted to acknowledge what we had, to be fully aware in the moment of how good it was to be with all these people and to laugh every day, to spend my working life with people that I would have chosen to spend time with anyway.

Mick Lally, who played my husband Miley on *Glenroe*, was like the kind of family member who is simply part of the set-up, the brother who is always there but doesn't say much. He was somebody who respected privacy, and kept his own privacy. In fact, Mick would normally sit by himself on one of the high stools at the bar in the set for Teasy's bar, with his book. When he was in the group dynamic, he was chatty and fun, but he wouldn't be as effusive as me or other members of the cast. I liked his company, but two people less like a married couple you couldn't possibly find.

HOW THE LIGHT GETS IN

*'We are involved in a life that passes understanding
and our highest business is our daily life.'*
John Cage

Mick and I didn't have to be chattering with each other all the time – there was a silence between us that was full of understanding. I liked his presence and although I can't speak for him, I think he liked mine too.

If there was something that was bothering me, I could go to him, but I respected his boundaries and didn't push myself on him too much. I know he wanted to protect his real family from being confused with his fictitious, television family, and our time together was tempered by that. When we were in a pub, we wouldn't sit at the bar together and we wouldn't be too attached to each other in public. We never wanted to give the idea that we were real man and wife beyond the make-believe world of *Glenroe*.

He loved the bed scenes with me because he would just roll over and fall asleep in between takes while I'd sit there, chatting away with the crew.

We hated kissing one another! We were like a pair of kids. Mick would want to leave the kiss until the actual take and then he'd close his eyes and dive. I knew he liked me and I liked him and that was it.

I always felt as if my job on *Glenroe* wasn't quite real. It was like some sort of other world, away from my responsibilities. The real world was still the world of my parents, which I went back to every weekend to be with my father, who never mentioned a word about *Glenroe*, and who I knew still wanted me to be at home by his side. Over time, I began to see *Glenroe* as a place to run away to. I sought the cosiness, the warmth and the humour of it, the cocoon that was created once the soundproofed studio doors were closed. When I wasn't in that cocoon, I was torn between my parents and my life.

I never knew what Daddy thought about me being in *Glenroe*. Although he watched it religiously, we never spoke about it. Mum liked being 'Biddy's mother'. She didn't like when bad things were happening to Biddy, though, because she would have to see me being upset on television. But I think she liked the recognition that came with it, the neighbours talking about the latest thing that was going on for Biddy, or how well I was doing in my career.

I'm not sure if she appreciated the irony that I ended up playing exactly the role that she wanted for me in life – a farmer's wife, conventional in every sense of the word – while beyond the camera my life was anything but conventional and very difficult for her to accept.

Throughout my years working in *Glenroe*, I continued going home every weekend. This was my way of compromising, and for a good while, it was a compromise that worked. But as time wore on, it turned out to add more to my problems than it did to solve them.

I was living two lives – one for my parents, one for myself – but I wasn't comfortable in either. Leaving every Monday to go to work became increasingly difficult as the years progressed and my parents got older. I felt more and more guilty because I was living a seemingly carefree life in Dublin – on the set of *Glenroe*, out socialising with my friends or living with the partner I had found – while Mum and Dad were struggling with the farm.

Work provided an escape from the chaos in my head, but when the stimuli provided by the set of *Glenroe* were gone, when I had to function in the world outside of my *Glenroe* family, that's when my real troubles began.

3

Religion

*'I have decided to come home, not to a paternalistic God.
To the God each and every one of us comprises and
contributes towards. To a mother God, a child God,
a landscape God, a sky God, a God of elements
and endurances.'*

Suzanne Power, *Angel Journey*

The Song of Bernadette

LIKE MOST PEOPLE IN MY GENERATION IN IRELAND, I GREW UP in a very traditional Catholic family. We went to mass on Sundays and Holy Days, and every day during Lent, with me dragging my heels. We said the rosary every night, with all the trimmings. We abided by each and every rule handed down to us from the pulpit.

I've talked about Audrey Hepburn in *Sabrina* and Doris Day in *Calamity Jane* being influences on me, but another big one was Jennifer Jones in *The Song of Bernadette*, a film about Bernadette Soubirous, the girl to whom the Virgin Mary was supposed to have appeared in nineteenth-century Lourdes.

In the film, Jennifer Jones had intensity and grace, and a natural serenity that I really wanted for myself, a kind of a queenly elegance. I'll never forget the scene in which the Virgin appeared, bathed in bright light with her robes floating about her. She was otherworldly, the most ethereal creature I had ever seen.

From being an eight-year-old child who was unashamedly bored at mass and resisted all attempts to get me to sit still in the pews, I turned overnight into St Mary of Westmeath. I built myself an altar to the Virgin at the top of the stairs, with candles and fresh flowers picked in the fields, and embarked on a prayer campaign that consisted of five rosaries a day. I'd kneel in front of my alter praying fervently with my little hands folded around my rosary beads. My mother didn't know what had got into me, her little girl had turned into a tiny zealot. Previous to this, she was always telling me to stop watching telly; now she demanded that I did, in an attempt to drag me away from my altar. 'Mary, get down here young lady and watch the television!' she'd say.

I wanted to see Mary smiling at me through glittering lights. I wanted my own mystical experience. I can't recall how long this campaign lasted, but, funnily enough, the Virgin didn't appear. I was disappointed but from then on, except for a brief period in my twenties, I prayed every day. I still do, although I have swapped the Ave Marias for Buddhist chanting.

My mother prayed consistently all her life too. She was very devout and prayed with great care. I think she liked the rules and regulations of the Catholic Church because they gave her a framework for living, but she was also a genuinely spiritual person.

My father was also an extremely religious man, and very strict with himself, but he had his own way of worshipping. Mum gave out the rosary every evening and would become increasingly irritated with Dad starting the Hail Mary halfway through it. He'd be saying 'Holy Mary, Mother of God', while she'd be back at 'Blessed Are Thou Among Women'. 'The Glory Be to the Father' was often replaced by 'For God's sake, Larry, will you wait!'

Daddy was always last out of the house for mass too. I remember one Easter, Mum was in a rush to get to the church because she wanted us to get good seats. There was no way she was going to wait for Daddy, so she set off walking, myself and my cousins waddling behind her like little ducks, along the two-mile road into Delvin. This became like a little tradition, Mum setting off on the road for mass before Daddy was ready.

I loved the Easter masses because they were very theatrical. All the statues would be veiled in purple velvet and before the mass, all the lights in the church would be put out. Then the Pascal Candle would be lit to represent the light of Christ. I would be completely immersed in the pomp and ceremony of it, entranced by the singing and the colour.

Like everything else in Irish life at the time – our schools, our hospitals, our society – Catholicism found its way to the very heart and structure of the family. I think my parents, in keeping with their generation, were very much rule keepers, whereas I'm a rule breaker by nature. I try to stick to the rules, but inevitably I can't cope with them and wind up breaking them.

Unfortunately, the Catholic Church doesn't look upon rule breakers with too much tolerance and, as I grew older, I began to tolerate the rules of the Catholic Church less and less.

The Feminist Gene

WHEN I FIRST WENT TO BOARDING SCHOOL, IN THE DEPTHS OF my loneliness and fear of losing my parents, I clung on to Catholicism with the same kind of fervency as my *The Song of Bernadette* days. I prayed morning, noon and night, and tried to be as pious as possible. But as time went on and the loneliness waned, so too did my fervour. Still, even up till my final year at school, I always had prayer campaigns on the go for this, that or the other. And along with puberty came a growing need to connect to something spiritual, to experience something transcendent.

My religious activities weren't always devotional. Like most Irish teenagers in Catholic schools, even to this day, we would have religious retreats presided over by a priest. If the priest was in any way old we would sit quietly like the obedient little women we weren't. But God help the poor man if he was in any way young. Groups of us would sit together in corners, cackling evilly as we composed questions of the most embarrassing nature. 'Father, what's the difference between heavy petting and light petting?' or 'Father, what is sexual intercourse?' We'd happily sit there and watch him wriggle with embarrassment, blushing like a traffic light on stop.

I remember one retreat priest who sat down and gave us this absolutely grizzly description of the crucifixion, asking us questions like, 'Do you know how long it would take to actually hammer a nail into someone's hand?' and 'Can you imagine what it felt like when the cross was raised in the sky?'

They were probably pretty accurate, but he delivered his descriptions like the eager director of a slasher movie and we lapped it up, squealing with teenage horror. But, while slasher movies are about a menace outside you, we were led to believe that we had somehow done this to Christ. He died in this horrific fashion for our sins, after all. We were the killers.

Coupled with this guilt foisted upon us for the torture of Christ was the encouragement to be ashamed about our sexuality. We were given a book about proper conduct with men and there was one story in it that I will never forget. It was about two teenagers, a boy and a girl, who were found dead from carbon monoxide poisoning in the back of a car. There was an awful paragraph about how the girl was buried in a white dress, a symbol of purity. She had been improper with a man before she died, but nobody but God could see the black sin on her soul.

Amidst these messages, I continued to connect my inner spiritual need to the only vehicle for it that I knew: the Catholic Church. But, increasingly, there were questions to which I couldn't find answers. Questions that made me feel defective as the good Catholic daughter of Catherine and Larry Mac.

For instance, why was the Church presided over by men? Why was there no place for women on the altar, turning the wine into the blood of Christ?

My spiritual beliefs were something I couldn't be casual

about. When I tried to start a conversation about the tenets of Catholicism with anyone – be they priests or nuns, or my parents or other adults – I was told I should go to mass, say my prayers, trust in God and leave the philosophy and theology to the hierarchy. I tried very hard to follow this line of least resistance and every time I felt uncomfortable about something I heard from the pulpit, I'd tell myself that if it felt wrong or didn't make sense to me, it was just because I didn't understand it properly.

I wasn't a dissenter from Catholicism, not yet, but I started questioning everything. I was too young to be involved, but I vaguely remember the whole contraception debate. The Pope, we were told from the pulpit, had spoken infallibly on contraception and he said using it was a sin.

Even though the actual use of contraception couldn't have been further from my experience, I can remember thinking, 'That's weird. He's a man. He's celibate. What would he know?'

As my years in school drew to a close, I became more and more concerned with the lack of a female voice in the Church. I wanted a strong female role model from religion, but there wasn't one, unless you counted martyred saints and the ethereal Blessed Virgin whose passive piety was supposed to be a beacon for every Catholic woman, but who didn't correspond to real life in the slightest.

I think that along with the depression gene, I also must have come into the world with the feminist gene. I was 18

Religion

'God is love, but get it in writing.'
Gypsy Rose Lee

when I decided that the Church couldn't speak for me because I was a woman.

In Irish society at that time, the function of women was to marry, breed a succession of little Catholics, stay at home, wear their best clothes to mass and bake buns for parish sales of work. The sad thing was that so many women felt they had no choice but to accept that fate. They may have wanted to be free to make their own decisions but, far from there being any support for them, they were told that even to want to be anything more than a producer of babies was sinful.

A few years ago, I got talking to a wonderful, spirited woman from my mother's generation, who had had 16 children. Despite the effect that being pregnant constantly was having on her health, she was encouraged by her local priest to have more babies. In the end, she suffered irreparable damage to her heart.

This woman loved each and every one of her children fiercely, but by God was she angry at the Church's interference with her reproductive system. She was the first woman of that generation I had ever spoken to of such things. I could feel her bristling rage at the inhumane rules that had caused her to suffer, and I was totally inspired by her courage to speak out.

Here was someone from the generation before mine who, without any support, had the strength of character to realise that the Church's attitude to and treatment of women were wrong, and she wasn't afraid to say so. It would be many years before I would muster up the same strength of character, but, for now, at least, I felt vindicated.

Back in boarding school, another element began to influence my increasing feelings that the Catholic Church was out of step. It was the seventies, and the hippie era was in its heyday in places like San Francisco. Its influence was even beginning to trickle through to regional Ireland. With hippiedom came the trend of transcendental awareness and interest in finding that spiritual state. But in comparison to people like the Maharishi, the Pope's brand of spiritual connection was somewhat less than trendy.

In sixth year, a day girl smuggled a magazine into us about the Jesus People, or as the world came to know them, the Jesus Freaks. They went about in multicoloured buses and their message was all about worshipping Jesus positively and free love. The lads had long hair and sandals and the girls had flowing dresses and crowns of daisy-chained flowers. To the eyes of a convent girl, they looked amazingly tantalising. So I decided I was a Jesus Freak.

I couldn't wear the flowing clothes because I was still in my school uniform, and free love was not an option because I hadn't the slightest clue about boys. My Jesus-freakery was purely on the internal plane, where God and hippies danced in happy-clappy unison, and it lasted only a few months.

I didn't know what I was looking for, but it was something

outside my experience. It was a desire to come to some kind of rest spiritually, I suppose, and a genuine desire to know God. I felt instinctively that there was something outside of myself, a greater power, and I was determined to know what it was.

Try Anything Once

WHEN I LEFT HOME FOR DUBLIN FOR THE FIRST TIME, I BEGAN exploring different religions.

The age of the hippy had well and truly come to the city and everywhere there were glimpses of alternative ways of living to the one proscribed by the Catholic Church.

There was a fruit shop on Mary Street called Green Acres that had a book section containing lots of spiritual publications. I bought a book of guided meditations and read it from cover to cover. It was mostly Eastern in its philosophies, but in each chapter there was a paragraph quoted from people in all walks of life, from Helen Keller to Einstein to Buddha, about self-knowledge and transcendental experiences.

It was a wonderful book. I tried to do all the meditations in it, even if my mind couldn't quite settle down, and then I bought more books, on everything from Sufism to Taoism and Zen Buddhism.

Although it would be seen as a small thing now, in an act of huge (if secret) rebellion, I stopped going to mass. Except for when I was at home in Delvin. There, all through my twenties, I would attend mass with Mum and Dad on my weekends home – always trying to be the good daughter I imagined I truly wasn't. But I really don't think I was fooling them. As time went on, it became quite evident that my heart wasn't in it.

Maybe I should have just come out as a lapsed Catholic, but I just couldn't do it. I knew the upset it would have caused my parents, and, as far as I was concerned, just me being me had already caused them enough trouble. So I kept up appearances, all the while continuing to search for a belief system that made sense to me.

The first time I had returned from Dublin to work on the farm, that search had come to an abrupt end. Indeed, during that time, everything of a spiritual nature died inside me. I didn't believe in Catholicism, but I didn't believe in anything else either. For the five years I was at home, there was no prayer, there was no meditation, there was no enjoyment in nature, there was a void inside me that I couldn't even begin to contemplate filling. It's hardly a surprise, given how important spirituality is to my life, that I became depressed.

For a long time after that, even after I returned to Dublin and my acting career took off, I didn't reconnect to the very strong part of myself that seeks spiritual connection. It was there, I could feel it, but I couldn't find a way to lift myself out of the religious inertia that had settled over me while I had been at home. I went to lots of different meetings about the Eastern religions I was drawn to, listened to lots of lectures and sat in lots of meditations, but somehow I couldn't regain the rosary-saying passion of my youth. I was literally dispirited, and it all just seemed like hard work.

Then one day at the beginning of January 1988, I was reading a Sunday newspaper. Being the New Year, the lifestyle section had a big feature about making New Year's resolutions. There among the articles about detoxing and weight loss was a small paragraph about Buddhist chanting and its capacity to cleanse someone spiritually. The practice advocated by the article was easy, requiring only five minutes a day, morning and evening, so on the basis of trying anything once, I decided to give it a go.

I chanted for a fella. Six weeks later, I was still blue in the face chanting and there was no sign of him at all. But, by this stage, I was enjoying the routine of chanting every day, so instead of giving it up, I decided to chant for a man who was right for my life instead. There were no stipulations or expectations. I just threw it out to the universe, figuring it knew better than my ego who was right for me.

Within a week I met Garvan, the love of my life to this day. It felt like everything – from the moment I started chanting for this man, to the moment I met him – had followed a pattern of my own creation, ensuring that I would be in that particular place at that time.

I knew him already through the music scene. He's a session musician who played bass with many of the bands I went to see, including The Fleadh Cowboys, Metropolis and Naïma.

But this particular night, when we got chatting, I knew something was happening on a deeper level. We both knew. Our relationship developed from there and we're still together over two decades later.

He had been separated for a year when we met. This was something I had no judgement about, but it wasn't so for my mother. In her eyes, he was still a married man and therefore I was having an affair with him. It would be yet another one of my major diversions off the path that had been set out for me, the one that I found so impossible to stick to. And this lack of approval did bear down on me.

Pandora's Box

HOWEVER, IT COULDN'T BE DENIED THAT, WITHIN SIX MONTHS OF starting my Buddhist practice, I had found a wonderful new boyfriend, had lost two stone and even my mother remarked that I seemed happier in myself.

So, rather than stick with what was working, I decided I would take my relationship with Buddhism further, by finding a group that I could chant with. Eventually, I located one in Dún Laoghaire and went to a meeting.

At first, I felt as if I had come home. I loved the sound of many voices chanting as one and I met people who, like me, found it impossible to be casual about their spiritual beliefs. People whose sole passion was to make the world a better place and who worked extremely hard at improving themselves.

The type of Buddhism they practised was Japanese in origin, and it had been developed at a time when the religion was going through a reformation there. It placed huge emphasis on self-challenge and hard spiritual work, something that appealed not only to the part of myself that wanted to help change the world for the better, but also to the darker side of me that beat myself up for not being good enough. Soon, I began to believe that my five minutes of chanting every morning or evening wasn't nearly enough. If the people at my group could do an hour a day, so could I.

This was the key that opened up my very own Pandora's box. After my very first hour of chanting, I had a feeling inside that I'd never had before. It's hard to describe it, except to say it was like the echo of a bad dream that I couldn't quite remember.

It is only in the intervening years as I've become informed about my depression that I can look back and name it for what it was, but, back then, I wouldn't have called it depression. I just called this not being a good Buddhist.

I figured I couldn't be doing the chanting right. After all, I shouldn't be unhappy if I'd found the right religion, if I'd found the truth for myself. Over the course of the next few years, I pushed myself further and further to be a good Buddhist. Within time, I was chanting for two hours a day and attending up to three meetings a week.

HOW THE LIGHT GETS IN

*'You can never go home again, but the truth is
you can never leave home, so it's all right.'*
Maya Angelou

So Buddhism actually became like a third job. I put all these pressures on myself and also I had no defence against people who would put pressure on me. I didn't have that sense of a boundary where I could say, 'Look, actually that's too much. I can't do an hour chanting with you tonight because I have to get up at seven o'clock tomorrow and do a full day's shoot before driving to Delvin.' Instead, I tried to take it all on. I imagined that if I did it all, and then some more, it would surely lead to the happiness I craved.

Some fellow practitioners, no doubt seeing the strain my practice was having on me, gave me plenty of gentle guidance to do less, but I was more comfortable listening to the people in the group who told me I wasn't doing enough.

The depression that had begun with my first hour of chanting became a constant state, but I convinced myself that if I could just hang in there and keep doing as much as I could, I would have a breakthrough. I continued to berate myself, trying to pray my way out of unhappiness, not realising I had a condition that, ultimately, would need medical intervention.

On a break from filming *Glenroe*, I went to Japan on a Buddhist group trip. In the magnificent city of Hiroshima, we were brought out to dinner with some Japanese Buddhists, and I ended up sitting beside this woman who was high up in the organisation.

During our conversation, she said, 'When people start practising this kind of Buddhism, usually we have to tell them to do more. With you, I think you should do less. I think you need to relax.'

I wished I had the dictaphone so I could go back and play it to the people in my Buddhist group from whom I felt pressure, because I didn't feel able to say this for myself, to defend myself. Throughout my life, there has been a pattern of putting myself in situations involving a lot of external pressure, then failing to equip myself with the defences I needed to cope. Ask me to jump through a hoop and I'll try my hardest to do it, even if the effort is detrimental to myself.

When the panic attacks started, I realised something had to give. I couldn't give up work, I couldn't give up my parents, so I had to give up my Buddhist responsibilities. It was a very difficult decision and I expected a huge swat from the universe for my lack of spiritual backbone, but I left the group nonetheless.

But the universe didn't react adversely and, after a while, I came to an uneasy peace with my decision. I continued to chant on my own and from time to time, I chanted with other people, but the huge workload was gone.

I have never been sorry that I made that decision. My fellow Buddhists were truly good people and I miss them very much, but I'm more at ease being a lone wolf. After a period on medication, I calmed down and realised that my lack of sense of self led to me using Buddhism as another whip to beat myself up with. Being in a very motivated group hadn't helped me find the space to discover a much-needed sense of self, it had provided me with even more ways to try and please others and be approved of.

The True Function of Prayer

PEOPLE SOMETIMES ASK WHY BUDDHISM DIDN'T HELP WITH MY depression. There is a belief out there that if someone practices a religion devoutly, particularly one of the esoteric Eastern religions, then they will rise above everyday troubles, come to positive conclusions about their problems, and be exemplary human beings who never say, do, or think anything bad.

However, I don't think of my Buddhist chanting as some magical cure for my depression, or for my flawed humanity. Of course I bring problems and worries to my altar and sometimes I do get answers, but I believe the true function of prayer is to gain an intimacy with life.

Let me try to explain what I mean by this, though language is a hopelessly inadequate tool when it comes to the parts of us that are inexpressible. If I try to describe a spiritual experience, I always think I sound a bit bonkers. To paraphrase Eckhart Tolle, the spiritual teacher and author of *The Power of Now*, how can five vowels and 26 consonants encapsulate the mysteries of the universe?

Despite the wisdom of Tolle's words, and at the risk of sounding like a complete lunatic, I'm going to try to explain the mystery of how religion works for me.

I do not believe that my life is a series of constant and random events with me at its centre. Instead, I am like one thread in an immensely large, mysterious and constantly changing cosmic tablecloth. Because I am a thread, I cannot see my part in the tablecloth's pattern.

I am a thread in the tablecloth, but I am made up of a series of strands. One of these strands is called 'the ego'. The ego is a very driven and creative strand and, if it is not trained well, it starts to think that it can see the pattern of the tablecloth and, therefore, define it.

That's where the trouble starts. The ego has its own defined idea of what the pattern is. Being the ego, it thinks it's absolutely right, so rather than accept that the pattern is constantly shifting, it insists the pattern stay the same, always. This is an impossible request, so the ego starts to become dissatisfied.

The ego asks, 'Why can't life be the way I want it to be? Why can't I have what I want? Why don't my dreams come true?' When the answers to these questions are not forthcoming and the pattern shifts yet again, the ego complains, 'Life is not fair.'

I think that prayer and spiritual practice are an attempt to tame the ego, to let it continue to be driven and creative, but to show it that it is not the only strand in the thread and its view of the pattern isn't the whole pattern, so it can never be in control.

The ego is very wily and can be off doing its own thing before you even notice, so the practice of prayer or chanting needs to be very diligent.

Now back to the thread that is me, woven into the cosmic tablecloth. The thread has many other strands: it has goodness, evil, kindness, nastiness, happiness, sadness and every other human trait you can imagine. Spiritual practice also works on those stands, strengthening what needs to be strengthened and keeping the harmful strands in check. In my opinion, we don't get rid of the 'bad strands'. We seek to transform them, while using them as weights to strengthen our spiritual muscles.

I realise that in the analogy department I have strayed out of the sewing room and into the gym, but that's the problem with reality – it won't sit still long enough to be defined.

So to finish with the needlework, when the ego strand has been tamed and taken its rightful place in the tablecloth, it becomes aware of all the other threads with which it is entwined. Instead of trying to exist alone, it realises that

'I have a hammock disposition:
committed to the air but staked to the ground.'
Suzanne Power

although it cannot see the entire tablecloth, it is enough to have faith that the pattern is right at any one time, even though it is changing at every moment. Now the thread can do its best to work with the other threads to make their part of the beautiful pattern richer and more colourful.

A Monopoly on Truth

IN 1985, JUST BEFORE I FOUND BUDDHISM FOR THE FIRST TIME, the first divorce referendum took place in Ireland. During the lead-up to the vote, I was at Sunday mass with my mother in Delvin and, during his sermon, the elderly priest said to his congregation, 'If you vote for divorce, God will turn his back on you. There is such a thing as forgiveness in the world, but in this case there will be none.'

For people from my mother's generation, this was a terrifying prospect. They were brought up to believe absolutely in an eternal life where you could be sent to heaven or hell after death, based on whether or not you followed the rules of the Catholic Church.

Although I was indoctrinated from childhood to believe in the same notion, without anything such as proof of fact, this was the last straw for me and the Church. I didn't agree with the problem they had with sex before marriage. I didn't agree with their take on contraception. I didn't believe in their pontificating about divorce. I couldn't accept the lack of an authoritative female voice.

As far as I am concerned, following rules is secondary to loving people, to caring about people and to caring about yourself. As far as the hierarchy of the Catholic Church is concerned, the opposite often seems to be the case, and often the spiritual message is simply lost to a succession of rules and regulations. Rules and regulations which, as the Murphy and Ryan reports exposed, have been bent, broken and abused when it has suited the Church's ends.

But to return briefly to the analogy of the thread in the cosmic tablecloth, once the thread that is the ego gets involved in religion, it wants to make the religion an image of itself, rather than reflecting its true image. The Catholic hierarchy tends to make God in their likeness rather than striving to make them themselves in God's likeness. To some extent, I think this is true of all religions.

But no religion can hold a monopoly on truth. The reason I started to practise Buddhism, and continue to do so, is because it would appear to be the spiritual frequency on which I can best broadcast and receive. For someone else, it may be Hinduism, for another Islam, for another the Church of Ireland. It is not for me or anyone to say what the right frequency is, although many people who practise religion allow their egos to dictate what that frequency should be.

When you consider the immensity of time and space, it seems daft for anyone to claim to have a monopoly on truth.

How can little beings on a little planet hurtling through a galaxy, which is only one of countless other galaxies in the universe, presume to have the definitive knowledge of God?

The nature of life is to be mysterious. If you can, make peace with the fact that you are not entitled to an easy ride. The more we can embrace life simply as it is, with all its difficulties, the easier the ride will be.

On the surface, my condition of depression is a bad thing. It's certainly unpleasant and I would prefer not to suffer in this way, but it is nonetheless one of that strands of my being and it has made me a deeper and, I hope, a more understanding person. It has a positive function.

One of the problems of depression is that it tends to blur all the lines in your life – to spill over into areas where it is unwelcome and has no role. Sometimes it can feel as if you're wibbly-wobbly all of the time. For me, chanting at the beginning and end of the day threads my life together, helps to contain it. Today, I do still suffer from depression, but I do so from a place that has some structure, from a place where I can exert some self-control, so my condition doesn't go spinning off into black infinity.

But in the very early days of suffering with depression, there were times when I would start my chanting literally on the ground in front of my altar, crying my eyes out. By time I finished, I would be ready to go to work. It was as simple as that. At the time, it was the least that I could do.

Letting Go

So, HAVING GIVEN UP ENTIRELY ON CATHOLICISM WITH THE advent of the first divorce referendum, I found myself, for the first time, able to speak directly to my mother about my feelings of disillusionment. I knew that, come what may, my mother would remain a devout Catholic until the end of her life, and that she would worry about my salvation until that moment, but we were adults now, and I felt that talking about it was the right thing to do. She didn't put up a fight, but she didn't agree with my decision either, so in the end we agreed to disagree.

I never speak to my father about my disillusionment with Catholicism. Although we were close, ours was not the kind of relationship where we talked about things that were intimate to us.

One Christmas Day, when I was 32, my father was ill in bed and I was lying on myself, reluctant to get up for mass. I still remember my mother silhouetted against the door of my bedroom, coming in, I presumed, to get me out of bed. Instead she said, 'You needn't come to mass, Mary. I know you don't believe.'

That should have been a moment of connection, where I threw my arms around her and said, 'Thanks, Mum', but instead I lay back thinking, 'What a cow I was to allow my mother to go to mass alone on Christmas Day.'

I wish I could have told her how much I admired her for making a decision that was so personally difficult. She never mentioned it again, but I know she struggled. As she saw it, not only was her daughter living in sin with a married man, but now she had given up the faith she had been baptised into too.

I couldn't stay in the Catholic Church, yet I couldn't reconcile myself with the fact that I had let my parents down yet again. Despite my best efforts, the deep seam of guilt inside me for not being good, for not being the woman I was expected to be, grew deeper.

I believe the way Catholicism was taught, by inducing fear and guilt, had a very negative effect not only on me, but on Irish society as a whole. We were taught to be ashamed and guilty because we were sexual human beings. We were told to be afraid of stepping out from under the Church's authority over all aspects of our lives. No one can reach their true potential or feel at ease with themselves when they are being controlled in the way that my generation – and my parents' generation, and generations before that – were controlled.

Each generation passed on their damage to the next one, over and over, until some brave people who had suffered unspeakable wrongs in the name of our Catholic God began to speak out. It wasn't until the revelations about the abuse of children by some members of the clergy and the subsequent cover-ups, that I left behind the sense of personal shame induced by my religious upbringing and the guilt for abandoning it. I know the exact day it happened.

HOW THE LIGHT GETS IN

'My soul can find no staircase to heaven
unless it be through earth's love.'
Michelangelo

I had the privilege of being on the panel of TV3's *Midday* the day the Murphy Report was published, on 26 November 2009. Our guests were the survivors of clerical abuse, Marie Collins and Christine Buckley, and my fellow panellists and I listened in horror as those two incredibly strong and dignified women told of the attempts by the Catholic hierarchy to shield the abusers within their ranks.

I felt my anger rising, not only for the victims of physical and sexual abuse, but also for the rest of us who had lived half-lives of shame and fear because of the control this massively flawed institution had wielded over us. We had tormented ourselves for our sinfulness, while some of those who told us we were sinners were twisted with cruelty, deceit and corruption.

I blew my top on national television that day, not in a way that might be remarkable to anyone else, but for me it was momentous. Without shame or worry about what my neighbours or the Delvin community would think, I spoke my mind about Holy Roman Catholicism for the first time.

I believe that Marie and Christine and their fellow campaigners have freed a lot of people by their words and actions in bringing attention to this dark chapter in the Church's life, and I, along with many thousands of people, am so grateful to them for their courage. They are an example of what Buddhism calls turning poison into medicine. Their suffering was immense, but by having the courage and self-respect to fight back, they showed many other people that they were not sinful, bad creatures in need of the Church's forgiveness. The Ryan and Murphy reports were a signal of a change in Irish society, a liberation from the clutches of a corrupt system whereby man had dared to try to be God, where the ego had been left to run riot.

If the survivors of clerical abuse had stayed quiet and had chosen to continue suffering in silence, all that cruelty and deceit would have continued and gone unnoticed and God knows how many more defenceless people would have suffered. In their refusal to be silent, they have also paved the way for different, more humble and compassionate Catholic Church.

To make sure that happens I feel the people of the Catholic faith must become more intent on influencing the decisions made on their behalf. There isn't a person out there who would not admit to feeling disgust and anger about the revelations of the Ryan and Murphy reports, but I wonder if we are making our response to these feelings visible enough. At the end of the day, we vote with our feet. If congregations calmly made it clear to the hierarchy that their time as latter-day feudal rulers is over and done with, if they absolutely refuse to be talked down to or controlled, things would change very fast.

But nothing will happen unless the faithful put themselves at the centre of the process.

As women, we have to demand that our voices are heard. Without women, most faiths, including Buddhism, would grind to a halt, yet none of these faiths truly reflect the needs and lives of women. The uncomfortable truth is that at the centre of how most religions evolved on this earth lies the male ego. And, when the male ego has its way, it is also an unfortunate fact that women get it in the neck. They are at worst excluded from decision-making, controlled and shamed; at best they are tolerated and ignored.

I remember a Japanese man who said to me once that when women are weak, men can be evil. When women are strong, men protect their happiness. I believe there is a lot of truth in that.

I don't think men are evil, I think they *can* be evil – the capacity is there in all humanity. But I think the strong do prey on the weak and I believe the world does suffer greatly when women aren't equal, when the rights of women are seen as of less importance than those of men.

In many countries, women are hidden away. There is a lot of talk about respect for women, but they don't have any say in public life and they make no decisions. That's because the male ego is dictating everything.

Buddhism isn't much better as regards the participation of women. When it comes to leadership in Buddhism, women are still rarely in prime positions, although this is changing. In fact, there are some forms of Buddhism where you have to have been born a man to become enlightened. Not even Catholicism came up with that little gem.

You may be asking why I am writing about religion and feminism in a book about depression. To answer, I will say that I don't believe it's possible to divorce how you feel from the world in which you live. For me, it was not only the family, but also the society I grew up in that had a huge effect on me. I was always religious in one way or another and I had an enquiring mind, so I picked up very early from the faith I was born into and wanted so badly to embrace, that to be a woman was, in some ways, a compromised position.

To Trust

I LIVE IN AN OLD-STYLE NEIGHBOURHOOD OF PEOPLE WHO KNOW each other and look out for each other. I really like the safety of being in the bosom of the parochial community and I treasure my neighbours. I love the idea that I know whose tractor is whose.

I have a stubborn belief in Utopia, in a world where everybody is in harmony with each other and with nature, and I try very hard with my own behaviour to create that in my community. I have never fought with other people. When I was younger, I was afraid to fight. I'm still afraid – but I also believe that, in the long run, nothing is really achieved by fighting.

I suppose my battles tend to be internal as I try to fight against the negative voices inside me, telling me that I'm not good, that I'm ineffectual, that I'm silly. I'm always calling myself silly.

But sometimes, after I chant, I go to the balcony outside the room where my altar is to do a little yoga. In my sitting pose, I look up out at the green fields that roll across the land, dotted with trees and hedgerows, and sheep grazing and the sound of birdsong in the air, and I feel fundamentally connected to the earth, to the sheer beauty of it. I don't feel silly or ineffectual – I feel part of the greater, natural universe, where no one is ineffectual and where silliness doesn't even register.

And I whisper my thanks to Mum and Dad, the people who made me, for giving me what I have. I'm the most fortunate of women.

In the face of the complexity of all the things that influence who we are and what we become, how can we live our best lives?

Some of us, not all of us, have a sense of something other than just our humanity, that we're not just collection of cells in a body. We can call that something Buddha or God or Mohammed, but, in the long run, none of us really know if that something exists. As some witty person once said, all of us who have disconnected from the Catholic faith could end up dying and going to Catholic heaven and being extremely embarrassed.

But one thing I do know is that, since I began to practise Buddhism, I have lived a more spiritual life and that not only helps me through my worst times, it helps me be the best I can be.

I used to feel that I had betrayed myself and the faith of my fathers by practising the way I do. There is a residue of this belief that never goes away and I must learn to accept it, that the things that made me who I am are all still part of me.

All I can do is trust. I chant and I trust. There are still times in my life when I feel overcome with an almost nihilistic sense of darkness and dread. But there are other times, when I get overwhelming signs of love and compassion in the world, and feel a sense of oneness with things. I wouldn't trade those moments for all the tea in China. They have been my backbone, through thick and thin.

4

Success

'It is never too late to be what you might have been.'
George Eliot

Being Biddy

TODAY, PEOPLE CHASE FAME LIKE IT'S THE HOLY GRAIL, EVEN though arguably fame, or at least notoriety, is a lot easier to come by than it was years ago. But if people have an idea of what fame brings with it, they usually find out quick enough that their ideas don't correspond with reality. They enter reality shows and next thing you know, they're plastered all over the cover of *Heat* magazine. They turn from anonymous people into magazine fodder, photographed by the paparazzi every time they blink and suddenly everyone knows their name along with the most intimate details about their lives. They might expose these details themselves because they believe that fame equals ultimate success, but they have no idea how living so publicly is going to affect their psyches.

Back in the days when three-quarters of the Irish population tuned into *Glenroe* every Sunday evening, celebrity culture in Ireland barely existed. Publications like *Heat* and *Hello!* were unheard off and would have probably been laughed off the shelves. So if you suddenly found that you were famous, it came as a shock to the system.

HOW THE LIGHT GETS IN

Within a year of being in *Glenroe*, I couldn't walk down a street in this country without someone pointing at me, shouting out, 'Whoo, hoo! Biddy!', and then breaking into peals of laughter as if they'd just said the funniest thing since Eve was a girl. It put the heart crossways in me every time, and then I'd feel like the village idiot.

Ask anyone who's had even a shred of fame and they'll tell you that being recognised makes you terribly self-conscious. It turned me from someone who would shoot the breeze with any Joe Soap into a very shy person. I'm less visible nowadays, but I still feel myself tensing up if I see groups of school kids walking my way. It's a hangover from my *Glenroe* days, when in similar situations I would be quaking in my boots.

A few years into the show, I was in Galway for the opening of the Arts Festival. I was getting into my car in Salthill when a whole gang of teenagers clocked who I was and started advancing on me, calling out, 'Howaya Biddy.'

I locked the doors on the car as they surrounded me and started to rock it back and forth. In truth there was no harm in them, just exuberance and drink, but I was petrified. Eventually, to my relief, they got bored and went off.

Losing your anonymity comes at a price. You walk into a room and everybody turns to look, nudging each other. They know you (at least they *think* they do), but you haven't a bull's notion who any of them are. It feels like your living with the laws of a jungle where they have all the advantage. No matter what happens, you can't be anonymous.

'You can't have everything –
where would you put it?'
Ann Anders

Little things that I took for granted were gone. I didn't feel comfortable going to pubs that weren't inhabited by showbiz people. I couldn't do my grocery shopping without someone coming up to share informed opinions about what Biddy was doing wrong with her fictitious life. Sometimes, I'd get people congratulating me, saying, 'Well done', and that was lovely, but that was not the norm.

Although fame is considered to be a kind of marker of absolute success, instead of making me feel successful, being recognised made me feel ridiculous.

In my dealings with the outside world, I began to anticipate bad things happening, at times experiencing a feeling of attack when people came up to me. I remember one day, when I was struggling with it all, a woman came up to me in a shop on Grafton Street. She proceeded to talk and talk and talk at me. I felt like I was being bombarded and, when I could get a word in edgeways, I politely made my apologies and hastily left the shop. She followed me out, and, as I walked away, I could hear her shouting up the street at me about how rude I was. I was really shaken by this.

Although it's often perceived that people pursue careers that are in the public eye, such as acting, because on some level they crave the attention it brings, I can honestly say that this wasn't true for me. I was a bit of a notice box, for sure, but I wanted to be noticed as an actor. Being essentially a private person, this new-found recognition didn't sit well with me at all. And the odd strange encounter, such as being shouted at on the street or cornered in pubs by people who thought it was great fun to pretend to be Mick Lally, really rattled me and increased by general sense of anxiety. I'd become famous before I knew anything about what it would be like. The genie was out of the bottle and there wasn't a thing I could do about it.

I now had to be very careful about how I carried on in public. One drink too many at a theatre opening and I'd start imagining headlines like 'Biddy Bladdered In Bar' splashed all across the tabloids the next day, fretting about the effect this would have on my parents when the neighbours bought the papers.

Glenroe was the nation's number one television drama for much of the eighties. Hardly a day went by, without there being something about it in the papers and every one of the cast became a household name.

Don't get me wrong. I was happy that *Glenroe* was popular and for the entire 16 years I loved working on that show, each

'I have learned to have very modest goals for
society and myself – things like clean air,
green grass, children with bright eyes . . .
useful work that suits one's abilities,
plain tasty food and occasional satisfying nookie.'
Paul Goodman

and every day. But the same time as I was enjoying playing Biddy, I didn't want to *be* Biddy. I found it increasingly difficult to deal with the division in my public identity.

The Vulgar Woman

IN *GLENROE* THE CAST ALL CAME FROM THE WORLD OF THEATRE and we just considered ourselves to be actors. We weren't television actors, we weren't stage actors, we were simply actors. And nearly all of us, during the three months break in filming, would do a play somewhere or other with a theatre company.

Although I find this very hard to say, I am a good actress. That's why people actually thought I *was* Biddy. They would come to see a play that I was in, thinking they were going to see Biddy, but two seconds in I'd get a laugh or a reaction, and I knew they didn't think I was Biddy anymore. They thought I was the character I was playing, which was usually an oddball, a drunk or a ne'er-do-well.

Unfortunately, so did my mother.

Would you believe that the only play I was delighted Mum came to see me in was *Charley's Aunt?* Brandon Thomas' comedy set among the British upper-classes might have been written in the nineteenth century, but it's been enjoying revivals ever since. The Gaiety production I was in was a big success and, even though mine was a small part, I wore a nice dress and spoke in a posh voice. You might have thought that Tom Murphy's *Bailegangaire* would have been the one I'd want her to have seen, simply because I shared the stage with Siobhán McKenna.

When I say that Siobhán McKenna had a goddess-like stature in our house, I'm not exaggerating. Mum once did relief nursing in the Aran Islands where Siobhán had a house, so I think she felt some kind of connection to her. Siobhán was almost mythological to me, right up there with Queen Maedbh.

Doing *Bailegangaire* with her was the pinnacle of my career so far, on stage with the likes of Siobhán and Marie Mullen in a play directed by the great Garry Hynes. The opening night in the Gaiety Theatre was packed with the great and the good. Mum was in the audience and although I couldn't see her, she must have stood with the audience for the ovation when we were taking our bows. Afterwards, she came up to me, but instead of congratulating me, she said, 'Why do you always get the parts where you have to use bad language?'

'As an actress, they are much more interesting parts to play,' I said, and reminded her that Siobhán used bad language in the play too. But she thought that was a different thing altogether. Siobhán McKenna was Siobhán McKenna, for God's sake.

To respectable women of my mother's generation, the worst thing a woman could be was 'vulgar'. I don't think Mum's criticism was about me not being good enough, but about me coming across as vulgar. I think she was afraid that people would get the wrong impression of me because I was 'fucking' and 'blinding' on the stage. It was almost like, 'If you behave like that, Mary, you'll never get a husband.'

In reality, the roles I played weren't vulgar at all. They were women who kicked against the traces. They were women who suffered through hard times with their heads held high and their gobs open.

Sometimes, Mum wasn't able to separate me from the character I was playing. In later years, she came to understand this separation, but through all the years I was playing Biddy, and working on the stage in between, I always wanted to play a part that she would like.

Yet on the other hand, if she had come up to me after *Bailegangaire* and said how proud she was of me, I'm not sure I could have borne such an intense expression of approval. I think as much as she kept me at a distance, I kept her at a distance too, because I often felt that if we expressed the intimacy we felt for each other, it would open a wound in me that I couldn't heal. Something that would make me even more vulnerable to the sorrow than I already was. It would bring me face to face with the unbearable fear of losing her. And I think she was the very same as me in that respect.

And yet I longed for that expression of her intense love. I wonder if she longed for me to express it too.

The Thin Veil

I WAS GETTING GREAT STAGE ROLES WITH WELL-RESPECTED THEATRE companies, with the cream of Irish acting. *Glenroe* was on top of the Irish TV ratings. I had just met Garvan, who was the man of my dreams. I was practising Buddhism, which was answering most of the spiritual questions I had been asking constantly since my teenage years, and, way more important than everlasting love and spiritual fulfilment, I had lost two stone! For the very first time in my life, I felt pretty.

On the surface, everything was perfect, but the cracks were beginning to show. Outside my working life, I was trying harder and harder to be the perfect Buddhist, chanting harder and harder. Little by little, a sadness was growing inside me. At first it was like an itch I couldn't scratch which was always at its worst in the mornings. By the afternoons, it had disappeared. Then, as time passed, it began to hang around a little longer.

I became hypersensitive to people and any careless remark would cut me to the quick. Up until this point, I had been fairly robust in the face of criticism. I didn't welcome it, but I could deal with it. Now, it was as if I had lost a layer of emotional protection and every little setback, those normal, almost inconsequential frustrations of life, got under my skin. Instead of bouncing back from criticism or getting over hurdles, I sank further into a vale of sorrow.

Initially, I was able to hide it by cranking up my volume. Outwardly, I was as confident and cocky as you like – Devil May Care Mary. I'm sure a lot of people thought of me as an arrogant queen bee: McEvoy had it made and she was revelling in every minute.

Naturally, people looking on thought I had the hide of a rhino, which is a very useful thing for anyone in showbiz. Taking criticism, constructive or otherwise, is part of the job and, although I don't think any actors are untouched by it, they can pick themselves up and get on with the show.

But I had lost all my resilience. Socially, I got the usual slagging and teasing, giving out as good as I got with good humour, but inside I was the absolute opposite. I could give it out, but I couldn't take it. It didn't help that I was a bit of a good-time girl, frequenting all the popular pubs and nightclubs, not an entirely advisable thing for a person walking around with a lack of emotional armour.

Many an evening I sat on a high stool in Madigan's of Donnybrook, at that time the RTÉ watering hole of choice, and listened, swaying slightly, as some equally inebriated colleague told me 'home truths'. Once, a well-respected journalist said to me, 'That's a lovely coat you're wearing, it would be lovely on someone who was a lot taller and a lot thinner, but it's still a lovely coat.' Another time, an actor from another TV show said, 'Oh, yeah, you're a fucking star. In a year's time you'll be shitting on us from London.' I would go home shamed and reeling, reliving the night and trying to figure out what I had done wrong to attract that kind of attention.

Of course, I had far more good evenings in 'Maddo's' than bad, but depression skews the ability to filter things properly. The bad is grossly magnified and the good becomes non-existent. Sometimes, however, comfort comes in the most unlikely guises.

One evening during the Dublin Theatre Festival in the early eighties, I was sitting with some friends in the Festival Club after being in a play. The club, populated with lots of other people who had just performed, was full of feverish energy. A lot of actors, myself included, need some space in which to go a bit mad after a performance. We are still full of adrenaline and it's like static electricity, and we need time to work it out of our systems.

So, there I was, crackling with this energy, being loud and, to my own mind anyway, as witty and fascinating as Dorothy Parker at the Algonquin Round Table. I was mid-sentence when a man I knew sat down beside me. This man was a figure of some importance in the theatre world, known for his sharp tongue, and he addressed some clever remark to me, probably a put-down.

I can't remember his words and I don't think that they were particularly or deliberately wounding, but something about the tone got me and, for the first time, my thin veil of defence fell. Tears welled up in my eyes and my chin began to quiver. I willed myself not to cry and managed to stop the tears flowing, but he had noticed my reaction.

I sat there, expecting a lecture about the heat and the kitchen and how, if I was going to survive in this business, I would need to toughen up quick smart. Instead, this man gently took my hand and spoke to me with a kindness and understanding that I have never forgotten.

His compassion gave me the validation I sorely needed at that time and I valued it even more because it made me think that, possibly, I was worthy of compassion, something that had never even occurred to me before that moment. He didn't offer solutions. He was just a witness who offered understanding and respect. In all the years since, we have only met once or twice, but there is always recognition of what passed between us that evening.

Time moved on and the sadness bedded itself down. *Malignant Sadness*, the title of the book by Lewis Wolport about the anatomy of depression, is the best description of what I was feeling at that time. It was a sadness that didn't know its place, deeming itself the appropriate reaction to every event.

One of my favourite Buddhist sayings is: 'Suffer what there is to suffer. Enjoy what there is to enjoy. Regard suffering and joy as facts of life.'

A Buddhist friend of mine once humorously observed that Irish Catholics tend to enjoy what there is to suffer and suffer what there is to enjoy. He wasn't far off the mark as far as I was concerned. I could do the suffering part very well, but enjoyment of any kind was gone from me at that time. I tried everything I knew to make myself feel better. I tried to party my way out of it, eat my way out of it, pray my way out of it, shop my way out of it – but nothing worked.

Because I couldn't fix myself, my sadness was shadowed by a sense of failure. I didn't know that I had already gone way beyond being able to fix myself.

Up to this point I had always had hope. It always glimmered for me, even if faintly. The constant effort of trying to feel better and failing killed what little hope I had left.

Through this dark filter, I looked at all the people around me who seemed to be getting what they wanted. Their dreams were coming true; their lives were happy and fulfilled. It was like standing and watching a carousel turning, with people sitting on the beautiful horses. It kept going around without stopping, and I couldn't get on.

Eventually, I started to think that even if it did stop, there would be no place for me on it because I wasn't good enough to be there. If I felt so bad, then I must *be* bad.

Have you ever broken down into floods of tears in public for no good reason whatsoever? It's mortifying. But it became the norm for me at this time. There were times in the middle of conversations when I would pretend to have a coughing fit just to disguise the fact that that I was about to burst into tears over something relatively minor. I would look at a tree or an animal and be distraught at their vulnerability in the face of mankind. The world became a cruel and dangerous place. Every day I woke up in fear that the people I loved would be harmed in some way. It was my fault, because my loving them had put them in danger.

Used By My Thoughts

AT THAT TIME GARVAN WAS DOING A LOT OF TOURING. IN THE still of the night, I would wake up and listen for the sound of his car coming home from a gig. My body would go rigid with fear, my heart pounding against my chest like a jackhammer as car after car passed by the entrance to the road where we lived. With each one, I became more and more certain that something terrible had happened to him.

Often times, he would forget to turn his mobile phone back on after coming off stage, so I'd get his voicemail when I called to make sure he was alive and well. The sound of his voicemail message would bring me out into a cold sweat, tipping all my fear of impending disaster into overdrive. Standing by the front window in my dressing gown, staring at the empty road through the net curtains, I would will his car to arrive into the driveway, delivering him home safely.

Each silent moment that passed brought with it a new and awful imagining. He was dead in a ditch on the side of some lonely road; he was injured and unable to call out for help. If he was travelling home from Northern Ireland, I'd imagine that he had been shot by terrorists. I tried to reason with myself, but my thoughts would spin further and further out of control until I was paralysed with abject terror.

There is a great quotation from a book called *Sunbathing in the Rain* by Gwyneth Lewis that I think encapsulates the disconnection with yourself, and with reality, that a panic attack brings: 'When you are used by your thoughts, your feet are not planted firmly on the ground; in fact you have no feet at all. You are only the shadow of a human being, blown about by circumstances. You there, with the wind whistling through your nightie, what is your original self?'

On those awful, sleepless nights, I felt as if I didn't have a self. At my core, there was only fear. When his car did eventually pull up in the driveway, I would scuttle back to bed before he got through the front door and pretend to be asleep. The next morning, I would act as if nothing at all had been awry.

It was a while before I managed to tell him what I was going through. I was ashamed of my lack of self-control and I didn't want his life to become all about coping with my demons. They were causing me enough trouble already.

It's very hard for the partners of depressed or anxious

'Remember this, that very little is needed
to make a happy life.'
Marcus Aurelius

people to do the right thing, or to even know where to begin. It's like the depressed person is an anthill: no matter how you approach it, you'll get stung.

Once Garvan went to watch the Super Bowl at a friend's house. I knew I was going to go doolally if he was late home, so I asked him to be back by midnight. He said he would.

About an hour before he was due home, my listening vigil began. I sat watching the clock like a hawk as its hands slowly ticked towards 12. When he didn't arrive on the dot of midnight, I began to pace around the house, dry mouthed and shaking. I tried to reason with myself but the minutes stretched out and with every one I was more and more certain that he was dead. He was never coming back.

What seemed like an eternity of terror was only 15 minutes. At a quarter past twelve, I rang the friend's house and begged him to come home.

Like any normal person, my poor man had no understanding that for me the stroke of midnight, and not second later, was the cut-off point for coping. The Super Bowl was playing out in another time zone, so he hadn't really been aware of what the exact time was in Ireland.

Home he came without question, bless him. I'm sure his friends thought I was one hell of a controlling bitch, and, in a way, I was. I had started to try to control others because I couldn't control myself.

In work, things never seemed so bad. I could unburden myself to friends over coffee, knowing that they didn't have to cope with the extremities of my behaviour when they went home. In fact, while relating details of my latest panic attack, I would see the funny side of it and what started out as a tale of woe from my increasingly insane inner life would end up the cause of stifled giggling in the corner of the studio. Indeed, we were constantly being told off for disrupting rehearsals.

My parents had no idea about what was going on, because I didn't show them. In their generation, everybody put the right side out, no matter what. Families lived their lives always thinking of what other people thought of them, and people did not admit to things that went on under the surface.

I know from talking to people, particularly in rural areas, that there is still a sense of 'what will the neighbours think' when it comes to mental distress. The stigma that surrounds depression is so great there is a fear that the family will be thought of as defective in some fundamental way. This stigma makes no sense. It is no longer necessary to lock people away because they have a mental disorder. There are very few mental disorders the render a person dangerous. I know people with all sorts of conditions, from depression to bipolarity to schizophrenia, who, with the help of modern medicine, live happy, normal and successful lives. They work, marry, have children. They even go into showbiz. They don't howl at a full moon or drink blood or run amok with a chainsaw. They are just normal – whatever normal is.

However, back then, I felt anything but normal. I didn't

fit in anywhere. I started looking for any excuse to prove my own unworthiness to myself, my own lack of value. I became terrified inside and I hid my terror away.

Depression, like anything else, has many hues and textures. In its severest state, it can lead to hospitalisation, or worse, suicide. But, very often, it manifests in a less tangible way – as a malady of the unseen self. You can carry on with life, even though you are suffering. To the outside world, you might even look as if nothing is wrong. Having an unseen illness is very inconvenient for us sufferers. If you have a broken limb, it's obvious – there are splints, crutches and bandages to prove its existence. Being broken inside offers no evidence, other than the mood we are in, and surely we can 'pull ourselves together'. The problem is, in many instances we can't.

This Court is in Session

ALL OF US *GLENROE* GIRLS WERE AT LUNCH ONE DAY WHEN Maureen Toal, who played Teasy, said, 'You know, we have the exact number of women here to be the cast of *The Factory Girls*.' Maureen had starred in the original 1982 production of Frank McGuinness' play at the Abbey. It seemed like a great idea and the gimmick of having us all on the stage together for this well-known, funny and moving play would be a great draw for audiences. So, to make a long story short, we ended up doing *The Factory Girls* in the Tivoli Theatre in Dublin.

Because the play was opening a short time after we had finished filming *Glenroe* for the season, the rehearsal period was very truncated and our press opening night took place without previews to iron any problems out, something that's usually unheard of in the theatrical world. Although *The Factory Girls* developed into a great show quickly, and attracted the numbers its producers hoped it would attract, on that first night, it wasn't ready and the reviews weren't what you might call raves.

Reading what the critics had to say about that play was the first time I'd ever heard myself referred to as a 'soap actress'. To my mind, *Glenroe* was never a soap; it was a very charming, rural comedy-drama. Indeed, people often criticised it because nothing ever happened, but I think that was the joy of it, because that's a true reflection of rural life. It's the simple things that people get craic out of.

I think Wesley Burrows, who created and wrote *Glenroe*, is a great wit and has such a gleeful, subversive attitude. It was the little things, the way he would phrase something, that might turn it into a wry double-entendre. I often wondered if he deliberately named Dick Moran as he did because Dick Mór translates as Big Dick. It wouldn't surprise me if he had.

But if the critics determined it was a soap, and I a soap actress, who was I to argue?

There is a courtroom drama that plays out inside my head.

My right to self-worth is on trial and the prosecution is winning hands down. When I was growing up, I was on trial for not being a good enough daughter. When I found Buddhism, the prosecution harangued me for not being a good enough Buddhist. As my success as an actor progressed, I was hauled before the judge for not being the right kind of actor.

On the question of my acting ability, the prosecution called the prosecuting critics to the stand. 'Do you solemnly swear to tell the whole truth and nothing but the truth, so help you God?'

'We do.'

'Is the defendant guilty of not being a good enough actress?'

'Yes. We have evidence that she is in a soap opera.'

In the dock, the defendant shook her head in disbelief. For the past 10 years, when she wasn't on television, she was on stage with the top theatre companies in the country. When she was on television, the whole country believed she actually was a person called Biddy Byrne, not an actress playing a character called Biddy Byrne. Does that not prove good enough acting?

'In the case of Mary McEvoy not being a good enough actor, has the jury come to a verdict?'

'Yes, your honour. We find the defendant guilty as charged.'

The moment I read the reviews for *The Factory Girls*, I realised the idea of casting the show from *Glenroe* had gone the wrong way. Having us all clumped together under the term 'soap actors' deemed us as somehow less serious than other actors. One critic, who should have known better, even went as far as reviewing us as our characters in *Glenroe*, rather than the characters in Frank McGuinness' play.

Although I gave it my all every night to packed and hugely appreciative houses, in my mind the verdict had already been passed, and I felt as if I was on a slippery slope.

Sometimes, when I forget to be compassionate to myself, I feel like I'm still doing time for the misdemeanour of not being good enough. For not being perfect.

But what I believe now – and affirm to myself regularly – is this: The idea of perfection is, in itself, fundamentally flawed. It does not sit with being a human being. We need to throw this unattainable ideal out the window and revel in being our own messy selves. Every one of us is scared, a little mad and a little fragile; some of us are just better at keeping it under out hats – contained, so to speak – than others. And maybe those of us who can't keep it under wraps need to shout out loud, so that the world will realise it is okay to be vulnerable. It is okay to accept our fear of failure. It is even okay to fail. Through failure, we find hope. Through hope, we move on towards becoming our best selves. Whatever that might be.

Then maybe it would be safe enough for everyone to let the mask slip. No prosecution, no defence: just telling the plain, unadorned truth.

Ordinary Perfection

THERE'S A FILM CALLED *SHALL WE DANCE*, STARRING RICHARD Gere and Susan Sarandon, which is a remake of a Japanese film of the same name. It's like Marmite. People who have seen it either love it or loathe it. I'm in the love it group, chiefly because of Sarandon's performance. She has a big speech moment during the film, about the nature of marriage and you can see that she's actually very moved by what she's saying.

It goes something like this:

'We need a witness. There are a billion people on the planet . . . What does any one life really mean? But in a marriage, you're promising to care about everything. The good things, the bad things, the terrible things, the mundane things . . . All of it, all of the time, every day. You're saying, "Your life will not go unnoticed, because I will notice it. Your life will not go unwitnessed, because I will be your witness."'

She could equally be talking about acting. Actors do what they do because they want to be witnessed, and I imagine that on some level, Sarandon is moved by this speech because she recognises this truth.

On some level, everyone is looking for notice. We are all looking for notice. I think this can be a positive thing when actors use it to explore the soul of another creature. You are given written words that embody a soul that the playwright has manifested. I picture all these little particles of soul flying around the universe. They come through the conduit of the playwright, who actualises their lives.

The actor brings them to life on the stage. Actors always think of their characters as real people. I would defend any character I play as if she is myself: I would fight her corner with the director. I think of it as quite a mystical thing. It's telling stories. All these stories are out there in the ether and you are telling them, via the playwright. Shirley Valentine wants her story to be told, so Willie Russell is the conduit for me and hundreds of other actresses to tell it.

If you see a really good singer, they let the song flow through them. The same thing has happened to me on stage. You do feel you are being spoken through rather than speaking. It's a very weird thing. It's like being hypnotised.

Since I've been vocal in the public arena about my difficulties with depression, people have asked me how I find it possible to go on stage night after night, often in plays where I'm called on to express the gamut of emotions, often through characters who have their own crippling difficulties.

The strange thing is that not only do I find it easier when I'm on stage, I actually look forward to it. Once I close my dressing room door to make my way to the stage, no one can get to me and I know I can give the audience what they want.

During my worst times, after the performance is over, I will scuttle away to the safety of my car, hoping that I won't be spotted by anyone in the car park. When the show ends, I know I have to create some space for myself to lick my wounds and heal.

Today, I don't have panic attacks. But I still get times of extreme sadness and unease. So far I haven't solved the mystery of why it needs to keep coming back. Maybe there's an answer, maybe there isn't. Maybe that's just the way it is.

All I know is that last summer when I was in the middle of an anxiety attack, trying my best to manage it by saying my Buddhist prayers, I chanted and then went outside to my balcony.

I lay on my back gazing at a blue sky that was dotted with scudding clouds and swallows that looped and coasted in the breeze. I could hear the lowing of a herd of cows who live down the road, on their way to be milked. In that moment, my world turned from frightening chaos into calm, ordinary perfection. There was a pulse of joy inside me and I whispered, 'Whatever You are, I love You.' It just seemed the right thing to say.

5

Loss

'What greater thing is there for human souls than to feel
that they're joined for life . . . To be with each other in
silent unspeakable memories . . .'
George Eliot

This is Life

I THINK OF DEPRESSION LESS AS AN ILLNESS AND MORE AS A PART OF life. We human beings, with our egos, don't like being made to feel uncomfortable, so we tend to label negative things and place them outside the norm, as if the only thing we were ever meant to cope with was ease and wellness.

While living from day to day can be full of wonderful moments and experiences, it can also be fraught with obstacles and difficulty. Whether or not we like to admit it to ourselves, loss is a fundamental fact of life, and one of its greatest challenges. Each and every one of us has to go through the pain of it.

During the run of *The Factory Girls*, my father developed a very bad bout of arthritis and took to his bed. It was one of several bed-ridden periods up to the end of his life. The loss of his vitality, of his power and engagement with life on the farm, must have been a bitter pill to swallow, and, during that time, I think he was suffering from depression. But, as with many families in Ireland, this was just not something anyone spoke about out loud.

Daddy was always a towering figure, decisive and active, even into ripe old age. It was very hard to watch him lying there, so quiet and inward, in so much pain, and to witness my mother's frustration. If I had been torn between my life in Dublin and the farm before, it wasn't a patch on what I had begun to feel then.

I felt that by going back to my own life in Dublin every Monday, I was betraying Mum. She was dog-tired. It was a long, hard slog, taking care of the farm and taking care of my father at the same time, dealing with his inertia and his own dissatisfaction at not being able to be the active man he once was. Because Mum had been a nurse, she was deeply frustrated that she couldn't make him well. At times, she took her frustration out on me, while I did the same with my guilty frustration to her, and we fought like cats. I think part of her envied me because I could walk away from it, to all intents and purposes fancy-free, while she was stuck.

Well-wishing neighbours would tell me I was the apple of my dad's eye. 'Your father misses you,' they'd say, and my heart would break. An only child, with no siblings with whom to share the ageing and loss of parents, bears the guilt and fear alone. I did the best I could – in between finishing the run of *The Factory Girls* and beginning rehearsals for a new series of *Glenroe* – but all the time, in my inner courtroom, I was being tried and found guilty of being the worst, most selfish daughter in the history of Christendom, and my depression was slipping further downhill. I had my own life, but it didn't feel like my life. It started to feel more like self-indulgence. My real life should have been at home by my father's bedside, helping my mother.

I think that, around this time, anxiety became a problem for Mum, but I only became aware of that later. Although she has passed on now, I still talk to her, and sometimes I say, 'Mum, if only I had known what you were going through, I would have been more sensitive to it.'

The truth was that the biggest fear I had was the death of my parents, inevitable and all as this rite of passage was. Towards the end of my father's life, we became very close. We had always been close – though never in a mushy way, we weren't that kind of family – but now our closeness took on a form of an equality between us. I was no longer his little girl; we were adults communicating with each other.

In 1992, the moment I had dreaded since I first discovered you could lose the people you love, came to pass. My father died. He had been bedridden for three years with arthritis and one morning, as my neighbour put it, he just sailed off.

I coped surprisingly well. The presence and help of our wonderful neighbours held Mum and I up. The hardest thing to see was Mum's sadness. She always dealt with troubles

'Old as she was, she still missed
her daddy sometimes.'
Gloria Naylor

in a 'stuff and nonsense' way, but now she was truly grief-stricken. I wanted to reach inside her and pull the sorrow out. I couldn't bear to see her in such distress.

As the weeks went on, Mum picked herself up and got on with life. She had the strength and stoicism that was common in women of her generation. She did her grieving her way and I went back to work, feeling like a traitor. My father was dead and my mother was left alone managing the farm. What right did I have to be doing my own thing?

Life continued on and work came to the rescue again in those difficult days. I was glad to have the busy schedule of rehearsals and filming with *Glenroe* to take my mind off things. Many months later, however, the pain of losing Dad was still as keen as the day he had been buried.

A work colleague suggested that I go to grief counselling. I found a wonderful counsellor who for the first time in my life helped me become aware that I had a right to my own life. I learned to understand that though my grief was normal, it was made more intense by my sense of guilt and failure.

At the time, it helped enormously. I didn't exactly leave the counsellor's office walking on air, but I felt I had turned a corner. Of course it was okay to have my own life. Of course I didn't have to feel guilty or over-responsible. Once I accepted all that and started thinking positively, everything was going to be just fine and dandy. Wasn't it?

A Diagnosis

As happens with so many first experiences of counselling, you can come away thinking you've confronted all your problems and that you're well on the road to recovery, when often all you've done is just papered over the cracks.

The idea that I was a loathsome creature was so engrained in my mind that, despite the advances I had made, I just couldn't hold on to the positive outlook I had adopted since seeing the counsellor. More than that, I started recasting him as an incompetent because he had told me it was okay to be me, the fool. My counsellor was, in fact, a distinguished, highly qualified man in his sixties. But in my mind he became one of those wifty-wafty, new-age chancers.

How could he not have seen what a bad person I was? What I needed was tough love, from someone who could see how defective I was and punish me accordingly.

In Buddhism there is a principle called 'Oneness of Man and Environment'. Basically it means that your environment matches the state of your inner life. It comes as no surprise to me now that, at that time, I found myself surrounded with lots of people who were quite in agreement with my dire assessment of myself. I was advised in certain quarters to pray more, do more, take a good long look at myself and purge myself of my weakness.

If I wanted to make my life better – and my mother's life better and the world better – I would have to steel myself and become a better Buddhist. I had zero compassion for myself, so the only people I deemed worthy of listening to were the hardliners. Those bright sparks knew what an abject failure I was.

My depression deepened and I finally reached the end of my tether. I woke up one morning, weighed down so heavily that I didn't want to do anything apart from pretend that the world didn't exist. I decided that this was no way to go on living.

As an aside, in all the years of living with my condition, I have never felt like taking my own life. As a grimly humorous fellow sufferer once remarked about her own condition, I was far too considerate to kill myself. If my being alive was such a problem, think of the mess my death would make for everybody? Anyway, no matter how bad things got, my lovely naughty *Glenrovians* would always knock a giggle out of me. At least when you're alive, there's always the possibility of hearing a good joke.

It was around the time that a friend suggested I see a psychiatrist. At first, that didn't go down too well. A shrink? Are you crazy? Or do you think *I'm* crazy? I was already well aware of what was wrong with me – I was the next best thing to the spawn of the devil. Why pay a shrink to tell me what I already knew?

However, by this time my friend, along with most of my other friends, had become weary of my neediness and she more or less insisted that I go. She gave me the telephone number

'My house burned down.
I own a better view of the rising moon.'
Bashō

of a very eminent man in Blackrock Clinic, where there was no danger of me casting anyone as a wifty-wafty new ager. I made an appointment, gathered together what little courage I had, and went to see him.

I poured out my woes, the endless underlying sadness, the panic attacks, my father's death, my inability to please anyone, my guilt at not being what my mother wanted or needed – out it all spilled in one long monologue. When I had finished, the doctor looked at me calmly. Then he said, 'Mary, you have been suffering from quite bad depression for a long time. In fact, I'm surprised you lasted this long without collapsing.'

You know the way sometimes the penny drops? Perhaps it was his demeanour, the clinical surroundings, or maybe I was just plain exhausted, but I *heard* what he said, and I *got* it. Instead of being upset that I was ill, I was flooded with relief.

A doctor with the right letters after his name had told me that I wasn't well. If that was the case, maybe, just maybe, it all wasn't my fault. Maybe there was a reason, other than my shameful weakness, that I couldn't pull myself together. I could have jumped up and hugged him. Until his next announcement. 'I'm going to put you on a course of anti-depressants,' he said.

I didn't like the sound of that. To me, at that time, taking medication was an absolute no-go area. As far as I was concerned, tablets were mind-altering and dangerous. Besides, I didn't need them now.

The penny had dropped. I was just thinking the *wrong* way. I would now think the *right* way and I would be cured of the illness that had just been identified. A few more visits to the shrink and I'd be grand. So I thought, anyway.

One Night in Paris

THE GOOD DOCTOR GAVE ME A PRESCRIPTION FOR ANTI-depressants, which I stuffed into the bottom of my bag, adamant that I would never use it. I left his office with a spring in my step. A new day had dawned. I had got to the bottom of my problem and the only way now was up.

Over the next while, I pottered on, resolutely trying to stick to my new regime of 'thinking right'. I was still a long way from understanding that my depression had passed the stage of being a disorder of the mind. It was now a physical condition, taking over every bit of me. My new regime lasted six weeks.

My mind, exhausted from years of deliberation in my inner courtroom, no longer had the energy to renew itself and get back on track. I slid into the old pattern of self-hatred and self-flagellation. Eventually, I decided I couldn't live like this anymore. Not knowing where else to turn, I fished the creased and ragged prescription from the bottom of my bag and I took myself off to the chemist.

I remember sitting at the kitchen table when I got home, staring in silence at the tray of pills, each one packaged in its individual plastic bubble. I popped one out and swallowed it with a gulp of water. 'Okay, McEvoy,' I said to myself. 'From now on, not only are you a thoroughly dubious human being, you are also a drug addict.'

Throughout the following days, I went about my life watching for signs of change. I didn't know what to expect. Dizzyness? The shakes? Sweating? Flashing lights? Was I going to grow hair on the back of my hands and start howling at the moon?

Nothing out of the ordinary happened. I continued to take my pills every day, gearing up for a planned trip to Paris with Garvan, where he was due to play a gig with Mary Black and her band.

As long as I've had the means to travel, Paris has been my Lourdes – a place I go to for healing. Any time I go there, I return home feeling, for want of a better word, vindicated. It's hard to explain. Because of the bohemian nature of life in Paris, it's a place where I can allow myself to be myself, without questioning. Even a weekend there helps me to stop being pulled hither and thither by my ideas of what I should be in relation to others, for a few days afterwards at least.

This time, however, felt different. I was going there with people I didn't really know, and coupled with my worries about what might happen when the medication kicked in, I was way outside my social comfort zone.

Dealing with my depression over the years had made me very insular. Though acting wasn't a challenge, interacting with people in everyday situations certainly was. I was only comfortable with people I knew extremely well, in situations I could bail out of without too many questions if it all became too much. I loved the relief of returning to my bedroom after some social event. I'd close the curtains and wrap myself in my duvet, safe in this 'womb' where nothing could touch me and I couldn't screw up.

On the first night of the Paris trip, we were in a bar having some wine and I did as I normally did. I excused myself and went back to the hotel on the grounds of tiredness. I thought I needed to withdraw before I did or said something wrong in front of these people I was only just getting to know.

Safely back in my room, I climbed into bed, but I couldn't sleep. I turned the telly on, but there was nothing worth watching. I was feeling a little peckish, so I decided to rejoin the group and get something to eat.

Four hours later, I was still in the bar and, lo and behold, I was *enjoying* myself. I was chatting and laughing, and being quiet too, without feeling I had to fill the space with talk.

I was comfortable in my own skin – a feeling I had almost

forgotten existed. In the corner of the bar, a little band was playing waltzes and polkas. Garvan and his band mates got up to dance, and I pushed my chair out to get up and polka around the room with Mary Black. 'Around the floor and mind the dresser,' as they say in the country.

My musician was grinning from ear to ear. It was so long since we'd had fun together.

Depression is like a visitor in your house who doesn't know how to behave properly. He wanders freely from room to room, going through your private things, rifling through your joy, serenity and rationality. In the end, you lose the will to show him the door.

My experience of medication is that it teaches this visitor some manners. It shows him to his own room and he only appears when it's appropriate. You can be sad when it's appropriate; you can be happy, angry, up or down, in a normal way.

Here, in a Paris bar, I began to reap these rewards, as I felt the effects of the medication for the first time. The depressive way of thinking that had taken such a hold over me had been shown some manners. I had been abnormally sad for so long that the normality medication brought was blissful. From that moment on, it was as if I was living life anew. I began to re-experience and enjoy all the ordinary things that, for so long, I had been unable to appreciate. Also, happily, my panic attacks became a thing of the past.

A Lesson from Jake

OVER THE YEARS, I HAVE TRIED SO MANY THINGS TO HELP ME with my depression, it would take too long to document them all. Psychotherapy worked in the short term, but my mind couldn't seem to hold on to the lessons it taught me. Every new insight I gained in the therapist's office would soon be swallowed up by the darkness in my head.

These days, I take medication when I need it. I don't for a moment think that every depressed person should take medication – by no means is it always the answer.

Over the years, I have come off medication for periods of time, with my doctor's guidance. However, I have always ended up taking the pills again. For me, that's the plan that works best, and I'm at ease with it. But it wasn't always so.

For a long time, I felt shame about being on medication. Every time a story appeared in the newspapers about the over-prescription of antidepressants, I would rush to my doctor and ask him to help me come off them. He would oblige and, slowly, we would lower my dose. Things would be okay for a while, but I would always reach a point where the anxiety would start again and gradually build until eventually I had no quality of life.

I have tried everything under the sun to try and replace the tablets. Even today, after all the experiences and self-doubt I've been through, at times I find myself having a go at myself for what I perceive as my weakness. Each time I speak publicly about depression, I receive letters from well-meaning people, advising me that I haven't tried this kind of supplement yet, or that kind of alternative therapy. While I appreciate their attempts to help, there is almost always a note of 'tut tut' to these correspondences. The writers really believe that for all forms of depression there is a non-medical solution. I believe this is a very dangerous assumption. A lot of depressive states respond well to psychotherapy and other non-medical interventions, but others do require medical intervention, at least in the short term.

Finally, after years of wishing it were otherwise in terms of my medication, I am coming to a peace about this too. In middle age, I don't have time to hang around. I want to feel well enough to enjoy what there is to enjoy.

My doctor and I have discussed this at length and we both feel that I am one of those people whose brain can't manufacture enough happy chemicals, such as serotonin. Depression is sometimes a sign that our serotonin levels are low and, when the levels are low, dealing with the normal ups and downs of life becomes very difficult. Some people are traumatised by simply living day to day.

For those looking on at us depressed people, it may seem as if we are overreacting to life, making mountains out of molehills. We are. We can't help it.

In many cases, serotonin levels in the brain can be brought back up to normal levels by other means than medication.

But some people, myself included, can't manufacture enough serotonin naturally, so our levels need topping up. I believe it's something in our DNA, a deficiency we're born with.

It's strange that our society, which has become so open and accepting of so many things, still finds it difficult to accept that depression is just another condition that can be dealt with and lived with. Because I have been open about my depression, people often unburden themselves to me about their own condition or that of a family member. In nearly every case, these people feel isolated and unable to talk to anyone in their family or friendship circles.

I am still struck by our unwillingness as a society to look depression in the face. It is not shameful. It is not weird. People who suffer from it are not 'mad' and they certainly don't want you to 'fix' them. They just want some space.

I could also say they want understanding, but I would be the first person to admit that unless you have been depressed yourself, it will be nigh on impossible to understand what a depressed person is going through. All you can do is accept them the way they are. Leave the fixing and understanding to the professionals.

Here's an example of a very simple and effective act of acceptance. Some months ago on a very sunny day in May, I was feeling wretched. I was deeply lonely but I knew I didn't want to talk to anyone or do anything. I went outside and sat in the back yard, feeling sorry for myself. My dog, Jake, wandered over to my side and, having assessed the situation, deduced that there wasn't going to be any ball-throwing any time soon. So he toddled off.

In my depressed state I thought, 'Mary, even the dog is fed up and doesn't want anything to do with you.'

A few minutes later, Jake arrived back with a bone that, by the looks of it, had been buried for a long time. He plonked himself beside me and contentedly gnawed for the next 20 minutes.

He could have sat anywhere with his bone but he chose to sit with me and happily do his thing. It was a simple act of pure and easy acceptance. You don't have to sit with a depressed person and chew a dirty bone. Just don't try to fix them. Don't tell them jokes. *Please* don't tell them jokes. Just live your life in their presence and, unless self-harm is an issue, that is enough.

Ordinary Miracles

I WOULD LIKE TO TELL YOU ABOUT SOMETHING WONDERFUL THAT happened at my father's funeral.

Throughout his life, Dad had always had difficulty accepting my boyfriends, perhaps because he was so afraid of losing me. I had been with Garvan for almost 10 years when Dad died but they had never actually met each other. Apart from seeing my father in photographs, Garvan had no idea of what he looked like.

He sat by my side throughout the church service, quietly supportive. Then, when it was time to carry out the coffin for its final journey to the graveyard, a man neither of us knew came over, tapped him on the shoulder and leaned over to whisper something into his ear.

Garvan stood up and went to the top of the church, called by this man to be one of the pallbearers of my father's coffin. The man I loved so much was one of the people who carried the father I'd loved so much to his final resting place, even though they had never once been in each other's company. To me, it was a small miracle.

Of course it wasn't miraculous in the biblical way that we think we understand miracles. There was nothing that couldn't be explained rationally. But what if 'God' wasn't an unseen presence 'out there', beyond our reach? What if science and reason and rationality and beauty and innocence and health and sickness and joy and pain and life and death and anything else you can think of *were* God?

What if we aren't able to see miracles happening because we're sitting right in the middle of one? What if the simple act of living is miraculous in itself?

If we could stop defining ourselves by the optional extras that come with life, like status, success and things that can be bought; if we were prepared to go through the withdrawal period that would inevitably come when we chose to look for fulfilment within ourselves instead of outside ourselves, then maybe we could find the peace of mind we crave.

I'm not proposing that we become latter-day ascetics and go off to live in caves and eat berries. All the good things in life are to be enjoyed, not eschewed, but if we stopped defining our happiness by them, if we could be grounded in ourselves and not live in constant fear of losing status or success or things, we might just come to a higher understanding of what our real value is.

Here's another thing. If we didn't define ourselves by what we have, it would be much easier to share. I believe that philanthropy, or the true sharing of what a person has without the need to get something in return, is at the foundation of many ordinary miracles.

Imagine what would happen if all the billionaires in the world went to all the charities in the world and said, 'Here's a couple of billion, lads: we don't need it to buy another yacht.'

The American-Irish philanthropist Chuck Feeney, who gave away $4 billion to schools, hospitals, the poor, disenfranchised minorities and many other causes without revealing his identity for many years (thereby not reaping the reward of pride in his good works), had it right when he said, 'I believe that people of substantial wealth potentially create problems for future generations unless they themselves accept responsibility to use their wealth during their lifetime to help worthwhile causes.'

They say that money does not create happiness, but Chuck Feeney believes otherwise. In giving his money away to bring happiness to other people, he became a happy man himself.

To use the words of his own philosophy, he's 'giving while living'. Obviously, we can't all be Chuck Feeney, but that doesn't mean each person can't give in their own way. Niall Mellon's Trust, which builds homes for people in South Africa, is a great example of how ordinary people can give, in an authentic and significant way, to other ordinary people. I've witnessed friends return from working with the trust almost high from the joy of giving. If you give while you live, in even the smallest way, you can make good things happen and be part and parcel of change for the better. We all don't have to be billionaires to give, and giving doesn't have to involve self-sacrifice – it can be small acts of generosity towards another human being. There is no greater gratification to be derived in life. What's more, generosity inspires other people to be generous, so by giving we create a better society for everyone, not just the person we are giving to.

Every Little Thing

FOR A LONG A TIME AFTER DAD DIED, MUM CAMPAIGNED TO get me to come home for good and manage the farm. The sense of responsibility I felt towards her began to extend to responsibility for the farm too, as well as to the memory of my father.

Things that my mother had wanted for me hadn't come to pass: in fact the opposite had happened. I had changed my religion; I hadn't married, I was unconventional. And now, to add to it all, I was refusing to do my daughterly duty of coming home to take over the family business.

It led to a lot of tension between us and it's something I regret. If I think back to those years, when Mum was managing the farm week to week, there were times when I wasn't very nice to her. If she was listening now, which a part of me fully believes she is, I would like her to know that I'm sorry for treating her the way I did on occasion. If I had understood what she was going through, maybe I would have held my tongue.

What I realise in hindsight is that my mother was suffering from anxiety and that she had very few outlets to express it. Instead of understanding this, I would wonder why she was getting into such a fuss about things, and I'd get irritated with her for being so fretful over trivialities.

Today, I do exactly the same worrying. If somebody is coming to visit, instead of just sweeping the floor, I have to almost spring clean the house. If I have to be somewhere on time, I'm up at the crack of dawn getting myself ready in case I'll be late. Little things are big things.

Now, I'm not saying it was *Whatever Happened To Baby Jane?*

territory – I always loved Mum and there were great moments of quiet understanding between us. We both learned as time went on that, despite the differences in the way we lived our lives, we were more alike than not.

Everything Mum did, she did well, not that she ever gave herself credit for it. I would be the one saying that her needlework was fantastic or that her brown bread was the best in the world. She'd quietly beam with inner pride that she would never express aloud when I'd say to her that the house never looked as good when I cleaned it as when she did. The love I felt for her in those moments was perfect.

Poor Mum had to deal with her fair share of anxiety from me too. After Daddy had died, she got her own life, making new friends and going out in the evenings to play bridge. If I happened to be at home when she was out, I'd be worrying like crazy about her, unable to stop myself from calling the house where she was playing cards and driving her nuts. 'For God's sake, Mary, I'll be home when I'm home,' she'd say. But I'd still be worried. Having lost Daddy, I suppose I was now even more scared of losing her.

6

Sex and Love

'The best and most beautiful things in the world cannot be seen or even touched – they must be felt with the heart.'
Helen Keller

Three Hail Marys for Purity

SHAME WAS ONE OF THE ROOT CAUSES OF MY DEPRESSION. I HAVE wrestled with its insidious presence in my life since childhood. For my generation, shame was the weapon of choice when it came to controlling children, and was used liberally in schools and the Church, and within families too.

Although everyone was taught to be ashamed, particularly by the Catholic Church, I believe women bore the brunt of it, particularly when it came to sexuality. Since Eve was first reported to have tricked Adam into eating the apple in the Garden of Eden story, female sexuality has been viewed with suspicion, as a thing to be controlled at all costs. Despite feminism and the freedoms women have won for themselves over the ages, shame still reigns.

Growing up in a rural community and being a fairly precocious child, I realised very quickly that there was something murky about my burgeoning sexuality. Back in those days, Maria Goretti was the saint young girls were meant to look up to. She was an 11-year-old Italian girl who had died from multiple stab wounds inflicted by an attempted rapist, after she'd refused him because of her love of Jesus and her loyalty to the Ten Commandments.

Maria suffered a dreadful fate, that is certain, and her courageous adherence to her principles was heroic, but what I picked up from the constant retelling of her story was that the secret sexuality that lurked inside me was going to be my undoing.

Holy pictures distributed to us at school depicted Maria as beautiful girl with Disney, *Sleeping Beauty*-like hair standing in a cornfield, gazing resolutely to heaven. Her face held all the refined purity I so sorely lacked. Her saintly beauty shoved all my miserable shortcomings in my face and I was ashamed of myself for another reason that I couldn't quite put my finger on. Mission accomplished Maria.

I think it was probably during puberty that I really started to feel this shame, with the arrival of my first period. I didn't know what was happening to me. We were staying with my Auntie Rose, my mother's sister in England at the time. I was mortified but Mum was fine with it, explaining everything to me. 'You're a woman now, Mary,' she said.

'Will I be thin now, Mum?' I asked. I felt fat and awkward, and the idea of 'becoming a woman' seemed like something that might take all that away.

'Oh, yes,' said Mum. 'You will.'

Of course, life continued on as before. My transition into womanhood unaltered – I was still plump and awkward – was just another failure to add to the growing internal blacklist.

At boarding school, I was the typical, green country girl. There were lots of girls in the school from Navan town, which was more urban in its way of thinking. Most of my classmates had more experience of socialising with boys than I did. Girls would get letters from boyfriends and I thought they were incredibly lucky. Boys were like aliens to me.

It was a habit of the Loreto girls to go on a walk called The Triangle, which ran along the railway track in Navan. Along the way, there was a hole in the hedge that looked out on to the track, through which 'Archieballs', the local flasher, would appear with regularity. We thought he was the funniest thing we had ever seen. Talk about an Irish solution to an Irish problem, Archie's was the first penis I ever saw. No wonder I have depression!

There were lots of books in the school library containing stories of the ghastly things that befell courting couples who strayed too far into an occasion of sin. Anything could happen to you if you did something with a boy, from accidental death to social exclusion, but the worst by far of all these richly deserved punishments was, 'the shame you brought on the family'.

Looking back, I know that if I had got pregnant as a young woman, no matter how loving my father was, he would have turned his back on me. My mother would probably have tried to deal with it, but he would never have seen me again. An awful lot of his generation would have done the same. The family honour was all caught up with God and religion.

The world was changing, though, and I would venture that along with me, a lot of my contemporaries walked around with this ticking bomb of heady, youthful sexuality inside us, saying three Hail Marys for purity to keep it in check, hoping we could last until the day that marriage and children (in that order please) saved us from ourselves.

Of course, most of us ditched the Hail Marys when we left school and slid into the depravity we had been warned about, but at least for me there was always that echo of shame inside, making sure I didn't enjoy the party too much.

Experimental Kisses

I THOUGHT MY FIRST KISS WAS GOING TO BE LIKE CLARK GABLE and Vivienne Leigh in *Gone With the Wind*. Instead, it was an awkward, intensely embarrassing experience that left me cringing. My Clark Gable was a boy I met at a party all of us sixth year girls were going to. It was my first 'adult' party and I was very excited about it. What's more, I was determined to get kissed. I knew this boy was going to be there and, given his reputation, I figured he was a dead cert. When he clapped his eyes on me, I knew I was in with a good chance.

It came to the dirty deed and he leaned over me and nearly broke my back. No sooner were his lips on mine than his tongue was pushing into my mouth.

My God! Nobody had told me about this. Surely Scarlett O'Hara didn't suffer Rhett Butler shoving his tongue down her throat? Eeugh! I was disgusted. My romantic, Hollywood ideal remained shattered for a while to come.

When I moved to Dublin, a year after leaving school, that remained my sole experience with the opposite sex. I was so shy around men that I would become tongue-tied if I tried to speak to them. I remember being out with a girlfriend of mine and a guy came into our company. He was just casually hanging out, but I couldn't open my mouth simply because he was a man. I sat there staring at the floor, hoping it would open up and swallow me.

I had my first drink at Moran's Hotel, which had a great blues and rock session at the time. It was a half pint of lager and lime in a tankard type glass and I didn't want anyone to know it was my first drink. I was sitting at the table with a gang, wondering if picking up the glass by the handle would give me away as being inexperienced. Alternatively, if I grabbed the glass without using the handle, would it look like I was used to doing it all the time?

One way or another, the alcohol gave me the courage I needed to further my experience with men. In fact, I went through a period of drinking to excess because I wanted to be one of the lads, and a few fleeting dalliances came about. They were nothing majorly heartrending, mainly just experimental kisses.

And then, just when I was beginning to find my feet with

guys, I made my big decision to go back home and become a farm manager instead of an actress. Good girls got married and had children, so that should be my calling, and it would also make my mother very happy. In Dublin, I had dressed and behaved differently to the Delvin Mary. I was hip and bohemian there, but not so when I went back to the life I thought was set out for me. My dalliances with men quickly went by the wayside, and it was almost five years after I moved back home, when I was in my mid-twenties, that I had my first real relationship, with 'the musician'. We could actually talk about art without embarrassment, and that was a revelation to me. He signalled an end to my isolation, to my not fitting in.

Although we split up six months after meeting, the affair with 'the musician' turned out to be the propeller I needed to get me out of the rut I had been in at home and back to the life in Dublin that I wanted for myself. But it would be a long time before I let myself even think about love again.

Sex was nearly easier than love, because love was so unwieldy. I was 'pure', as the Holy Roman Catholic Pope might put it, until I was 21. At that time, I didn't have a clue what sex was all about, but I felt I should do it anyway. I think everybody of my generation was the same. We were growing up at a time when people were starting to question the Catholic Church's edicts around sex, but none of us had a template to work from because our parents were of a generation who blindly obeyed. We were grappling around, trying to find our feet, clueless about how to behave.

I think so many of my contemporaries lost their virginity simply to be rid of it – to get the whole messy business over and done with. I was no different. Losing my virginity was functional – neither pleasant nor unpleasant.

Once it was done, all I felt was relief. It didn't open the floodgates to love or lust. I was just delighted that at last I was a member of the non-virgin brigade. At that time, for girls my age *not* to be a virgin was a badge of honour. In a way, it was the sanitisation of sex. There was no romance involved, no feelings other than the desire to grow up. I'm sure that around this time I accepted treatment from men that was less than respectful, thinking that this was part of the process of becoming a proper adult. I didn't have anyone to talk to about it, so I had no idea of what my expectations should have been.

Over time, my relationships with men took a turn for the worse, and I began to become obsessive.

Marriage Material

I WAS NEVER WHAT YOU MIGHT CALL A STALKER. THERE WAS NO hiding in the bushes outside a guy's house, or telephoning him in the middle of the night with heavy breathing. I wasn't Glenn Close in *Fatal Attraction*.

My obsessions with guys were mild. I was more like a little

'Love never dies of starvation but often of indegestion.'
Ninon de Lenclos

puppy, following its master around with its tongue hanging out. Behaviour not abnormal for a teenager, but I was 28! I look back at the woman I was back then with a certain amount of sadness for her. I was very immature, both emotionally and physically.

I developed an obsession with a guy who worked in the music business. I thought he was only gorgeous and the one for me. I bumped into him one evening in town. He was with a couple of very famous international Irish music stars and they were on their way to The Pink Elephant, *the* place to be seen in at the time.

By this time, the first episodes of *Glenroe* had been broadcast, and I was in a show in The Gate – I was an actress with a capital A, so I felt I had some kind of 'in' with the 'in crowd'. It didn't cost me a thought to follow them.

When we got to The Pink Elephant, they took their places at a large circular table in a sectioned-off alcove, which was soon filled with drinks. When one wasn't forthcoming for me, I went up to the bar and got my own. Trying my very best to look cool as a cucumber, I went over to their table and tried to sit very languidly at the front of the table, not realising there were no seats. As I plonked down on the ground, I grabbed the edge of the table in an effort to save myself, dragging the whole thing down on top of me. The man of my obsessional dreams, along with two of the most famous people in the country, were staring at me like I had landed down from outer space.

Even now I blush from head to toe when I think about it. That girl on the floor of The Pink Elephant, soaked with alcohol, desperately trying to pull herself together and not look like an eejit in front of this man, had no sense of herself. She was following a guy around who hadn't the slightest interest in her, thinking it was all perfectly fine and normal.

At the back of my mind, all through this time, getting married to the man of my dreams was still my goal. I was always eyeing up somebody for marriage. I had received every bit of my training from black and white movies, in which there may have been obstacles on the course to true love, but there was always a happy ending with the two lovers walking hand-in-hand off into the sunset.

I wanted the big wedding in the white dress, and it had to be in the church at home in Delvin. I would find the person that I would stay with for the rest of my life; we would commit to each other in front of God and my community, and live happily ever after.

It was only when I found Buddhism that my ideas of love began to change. Buddhism isn't about being blissed out, it's more about strengthening your inner person so that you can become 'a capable person for world peace' – as in, a human being who is strong enough to have an impact on your society for the better, however small the impact is.

At the time when I first started chanting, a new love obsession was ongoing. In Buddhism, you chant for what you want, but the act of chanting in itself is the transformative thing – it doesn't really matter what you chant for. Having said that, quite a lot of the time you get what you chant for as a by-product.

I decided I would chant for a particular guy and it seemed to work perfectly. He asked me out on a date and we spent a lovely, romantic evening together, walking about town holding hands. When we were parting, he said, 'I'll call you next week.' That was the last I heard from him.

Despite this clear message of non-interest, my obsession continued and I chanted day in, day out for him to call me. Here I was, hoping for a happy ever after with a guy who didn't care that I existed.

Then, one day it finally dawned on me. That guy was not the right guy for me. So, from that morning, without any obsession in mind, I started chanting for the right guy for me.

I met Garvan within a week.

Picking Blackcurrants

AS A REGULAR GIG GOER, I'D BEEN ON A NODDING ACQUAINTANCE with Garvan, a bass player with various bands, for years before we got together. Then, one night, I ended up chatting to him about answering machines. They were the big thing back then, kind of like the iPhone is today. Both of us had shelled out on answering machines and we were lamenting the problems that came with them. 'The trouble with mine,' I said, 'is that nobody every leaves me a message.'

'Well, give me your phone number and *I'll* leave you a message.' He smiled and, in that exact moment, I felt a little heart-flutter.

He never did leave me a message, the sod.

A few nights later, I headed out to a gig and when I got there I spotted him immediately. He was standing in the aisle, watching the band. As I approached him, he turned around and put his arms out. I walked into them, and that was that.

We've been together for 23 years and every day I think how lucky I've been. After all this time, I still light up when he walks into the room.

Not that it's always sweetness and light. Just like me, he can be cranky and hard to get along with. We're human, after all.

I've learned a lot about myself in the context of my relationship through Buddhism, through trying to tease out my confusions by chanting. I remember a time when, in the early years, Garvan had been very busy with rehearsals for a few weeks, and we hadn't seen much of each other, even though we were living together. He had a break coming up and I had this whole romantic thing in my head. I'd arrive home from work and he'd be there. He'd sweep me up in his arms and tell me how much he missed me.

Instead, he was outside picking blackcurrants in the garden. When I went out, he looked up and said hello.

I was furious at the lack of fuss he made and I went back into the house and rang the leader of my Buddhist group and gave out hell, 'The bastard, he's out picking blackcurrants, can you believe it? He doesn't give a fuck about me!'

I have never forgotten what the group leader replied. 'Mary,' she said, 'if I lived with you, *I'd* be out picking blackcurrants. Relax about it. He doesn't have to do what you want him to do – go out and pick blackcurrants with him.'

Which is what I did.

It changed my whole notion of everything, helping me see sense in very ordinary things. Instead of losing it if life didn't go exactly as I'd planned it in my head, I began to go with the flow of what was really happening in the moment. Not attaching yourself to your great expectations gives you freedom to enjoy the unexpected little pleasures of a relationship, and of life.

We had a lovely time together picking blackcurrants, gently in each other's company. It wasn't about a great grand gesture; it was small, but real. When my expectations of life become too entrenched, I always go back to that moment.

I've heard it said that the most romantic thing you can say to another person is, 'You complete me.' If somebody says that to you, I'd say get the hell out of there quick, because if you're looking for completion in another person, you are never going to get it.

Sex and Love

'Grow old with me!
The best is yet to be.'
Robert Browning

We change all the time. We each have our own destiny, our own path of development, our own life. And just because a person is your husband, boyfriend, girlfriend, wife, whatever, they don't have to change for you. If we can't accept each other as we are, we may as well forget about it and walk away.

Over the years, Garvan and I have learned to accept that neither of us is going to change for the other. And it's not that I accepted him not changing. I just accepted him.

You can go from experiencing your love for someone one minute, to wanting to punch their lights out for saying something the next, then back to loving them again. If we try and convince ourselves that the purpose of a relationship is to carve out a smooth road together, we are in danger of self-deception. Ongoing harmony in a relationship is a rare thing. Every couple has their ups and downs. That's life.

Part of my journey is learning to accept the rough and the smooth, both in life and in other people. One of the things I cherish most about my relationship with Garvan is the companionship we share. He doesn't have to hug me all the time. He doesn't have to do anything. I don't even have to speak to him. Simply having him here is enough.

We realise we're very lucky to have found each other and to still be together. We take nothing for granted. It might sound strange, but it's almost like we meet every so often in eternity, just the two of us.

Children

GARVAN HAD BEEN SEPARATED FOR A YEAR WHEN I MET HIM AND he had a five-year-old daughter, Carla. She was a charming child, a little force of nature, and her father adored her.

As much as my own father adored me, he had still been a very distant man. Garvan was anything but, and, in some ways, I envied his daughter's connection with him.

Although I was in my thirties, in many ways I was like an immature child. I had insecurities about my place in the relationship between Garvan and his daughter, if indeed I had one. I craved a sense of my own territory, but because the man I fell in love with had a complicated life, the territory where I had landed wasn't always the easiest on which to find my feet. I tried my best.

Whenever I'm signing a card for Carla, I always sign 'WSM', for 'the wicked stepmother'. It's a joke between us. I don't think I *was* a wicked stepmother, though. I hid my insecurities from her because she was a child, and I tried to work through them to find my peace with the situation, which is what eventually happened. Today, we are great friends, and it is to her credit that she has never had a problem with me, not from day one.

I don't think it helped in the early days that my Mum was so upset with my choice of man. Guided by her moral compass, to her Garvan remained a married man – which technically he was, as divorce wasn't available in Ireland then. I was still in the frame of mind where I wanted to get married and have children and he couldn't remarry – and he didn't want to either. He'd been there and bought the T-shirt, and he didn't want to go on a return visit. It was nothing to do with a lack of commitment to me, he just didn't believe in marriage as a concept or an institution – and I respected that.

But I did want to have a child. Garvan, on the other hand, was not so keen. Eventually, I sat down in front of my altar and asked myself, 'Do I love him? Or do I love the him I want him to be?'

The answer came back. I loved him for who he was. From that point on, I accepted the situation as it was. Now I'm glad that I didn't get married and have children. I was already suffering from depression, though I didn't label it as such back then, and I believe that the responsibilities of parenthood would only have made my condition worse.

The one regret I would have is not having nieces and nephews. That would have been lovely. But that was out of my hands.

Depression and Love

I BELIEVE LOVE IS DIFFERENT FOR EVERYONE. FOR ME, LOVE IS about getting as much joy out of my partner's happiness as from my own, if not more.

In the Buddhist notion of relationships, you're two separate people with two separate fates, but there are ways of entwining so you can create something together. It's not about one partner's weakness being bolstered up by the other's strength, or vice versa. It's more about the idea that by working mindfully through your difficulties, you create something strong and inspiring for the world at large.

If you suffer from depression, you have to be very aware of how your condition is influencing your reactions and interactions with your partner. It's not always easy.

Sometimes when I am in the depths of anxiety, I get paranoid. In that state, I have to remind myself that negative ideas I might have formed about my partner's feelings are actually part my depression. They do not necessarily reflect the reality of my relationship.

The truth may be that your partner loves you completely, but it is a big mistake to rely on his or her love to wrestle you from your depression. What if love saves you and then you lose that love? Do you go back to depression again? The love of another is not a reliable saviour.

Similarly, the partner of the depressed person might think

that his or her love will save the depressed person from their depression. This is also a mistake. Depression is a condition. People suffer with it, whether they are loved or not. Your love may help the depressed person on a fundamental level, simply by being part of their life, but it will never rescue your partner from the clutches of their condition. The only person who can rescue the depressed person is the depressed person.

I think of my depression as being of the whirling dervish variety. Where others might take to bed, unable to face the world, I turn into this anxiety-ridden lunatic, running from invisible demons all the time, desperately trying to distract myself from the darkness.

When I'm like this, there are times when Garvan knows it's best to just leave me to myself. On other occasions, a small gesture can be a big help. Something as simple as saying, 'Just sit down for a second and I'll make you cup of tea', is enough to break the circuit of the electric current that keeps running.

The current of anxiety that can't be broken by someone else is the more existential kind, where you're waking up at five o'clock in the morning filled with negative feelings about yourself. No matter what happens, nobody can convince you that your thoughts aren't real.

In my worst anxious states, I just can't see any evidence that I'm a good person. I've become so knowledgeable about it now that I can often nip an anxiety attack in the bud. I am learning to break my own current.

Being in my relationship helps me so fundamentally that I cease to even notice it helping. I have no need to question. Garvan is my witness.

'Compassion' is a word that Buddhists use more often than 'love'. That all-encompassing love we see reflected in the dream world of the movies is understood in Buddhism as lacking in an essential way. The idea is to begin to look at your relationship from the outside in, rather than the inside out. You start to consider how it works. By detaching to a degree, you open yourself up to a realistic kind of love rather than attaching yourself to an unattainable ideal.

I still feel a physical heart love when I see my partner. I take no day for granted.

Loving Myself

THE OTHER DAY, I WAS AT MY ALTAR CHANTING FOR THE RECOVERY of a friend who had become ill. I genuinely believe that putting positive energy to work on her behalf in this way will bring results.

I sometimes chant for myself too, for a particular thing to work out for me, for instance. I am more sceptical when it comes to myself than when I am chanting for the good of another person, yet I still end up actually getting what I want and need most of the time. So what lies in the gap between not believing I'll get it but actually getting it nonetheless?

Perhaps what's lacking is compassion for myself. It is often easier for us to show compassion to others than to ourselves. Lots of self-help books tell you to look in the mirror every say and say to yourself, 'I love you.' I've tried to show myself unconditional love, but generally what I find is that conditions start slipping in. I can accept certain things about myself, but not others.

But the key to finding true compassion for yourself is, of course, to accept yourself just as you are. I'm on that journey. Now, when I begin to condemn things in myself, I recognise it for what it is. I know that it's up to me to change the record, and develop new thought patterns.

Everything is cyclical. A person who is feeling like shit may not be able to rid themselves of the idea that it's going to continue *ad infinitum*. People who self-harm do so because they want the shit feeling to stop, rather than their lives to stop. But things do get better, and we have to hang on to that. I have this lump in my throat almost daily because of an underlying sadness that never goes away. But that's how the light gets in. With it, I also have moments of wonderful happiness and joy.

Not a day goes by when I don't experience enjoyment, whether it is from diving into the lake for a swim, hugging my beloved donkeys, or having a good meal with my man. I believe it's an achievement to carry the sadness and darkness inside and still be able to have happy moments.

I woke up on a recent Sunday morning, stretched my arms out and thought, bliss, I have a free day. I'll go and get the papers and have a lazy Sunday reading them. It wasn't long before I realised this was a bad move.

It was nothing to do with the IMF or the recession. That stuff may bother me, but it doesn't depress me. What really got me down was the vitriolic tone of much of what I read: it seems that, increasingly, we get our entertainment through cruelty, through seeing people humiliated on reality television or through catty comments about celebrities.

I believe that the casual cruelty which runs through much of the 'infotainment' industry can have a numbing effect on our subconscious, at best making us insensitive, at worst making us feel unsafe. The abundance of media pointing out people's defects is creating an atmosphere of cruelty. If you read enough of it, you begin to believe that casual cruelty is all right. It's not that you might be cruel yourself, but that your subconscious becomes vulnerable to such cruelty.

If we are ever to be truly compassionate to ourselves, we must first learn to be compassionate to the world around us, warts and all.

'You'd worry less about what people thought of you
if you knew how seldom they do it.'
Olin Miller

My Sexual Salvation

I REALLY ONLY DITCHED MY SHAME ABOUT SEX WHEN I WAS in my forties and was asked to do a play called *The Vagina Monologues* by Eve Ensler. It was one of the strongest pieces of theatre in which I have ever been lucky enough to act. Based on the testimonies of real women, it examines these women's relationships with their own vaginas. The material is honest, direct and sexually confrontational in the extreme. In short, a tall order for yours truly.

Like many Irish people, I have no problem telling dirty jokes (as long as they're funny), and living in the country has given me a good line in earthy ribaldry, but I find talking about sex in a normal, direct way, toe-curlingly embarrassing.

My French friends always amaze me when they discuss sex. Contrary to the stereotype, they don't spend hours discussing *l'amour*, but when they do, they are direct and unabashed. Sex is just a natural function for them. Talking about it is just as ordinary.

The shame I felt during puberty about that most integral part of my humanity created a sense of isolation within me that undoubtedly added to the causes of my depression.

The fact that Biddy, my TV persona, wasn't exactly a paragon of sexual liberation didn't help. Biddy was the patron saint of thermal vests and sensible knickers and unfortunately in the public eye, we were aligned.

In a way, *The Vagina Monologues* was my sexual salvation. If I was to give a truthful performance, I would have to confront the shame monster. The production was very theatrical, with a huge red silk backdrop and the cast – myself, Dillie Keane and Twink – were dressed in glamorous black dresses. My dress was one that I would have killed to wear as a young Audrey Hepburn fan. Yet here I was, fat, forty and utterly unsuited to such glamour, in my own estimation at least. I had mixed feelings when I put it on at first. I loved the dress, but I wasn't so happy about my body in it.

There comes a time in a play when you have to toss any misgivings you have over your shoulder and just get out there to do your job. My first night was inauspicious. The set was bare except for three stools – three very high stools I might add. Us girls were supposed to walk out, get on the stools and start the show when the lights came up.

I am not very tall. As they say in Westmeath, I should have sued the council for building the road too close to my arse, so those vertiginous stools were a bit, shall we say, problematic.

When the lights came up I was still trying to clamber on to my fecking stool, back to the audience and bum in the air. The stool swayed side to side, threatening to knock my fellow cast members of theirs.

I had no choice but to play it for laughs, red-faced and sweating from exertion and embarrassment. Other short-arsed actresses would have foreseen this situation and asked for a little footstool to negate the problem, but I think that subconsciously I chose to be clumsy and ungainly. It was easier accessing the ham-fisted part of myself, rather than stepping out into the limelight and being the Cinderella I had always wanted to be. I still hadn't realised that I had the right to step into myself as an attractive woman.

Despite that tricky start, I came to love *The Vagina Monologues* and revelled in the new challenges of being outrageous. Not that the show itself is outrageous in any way, but it *felt* outrageous to sit there revealing the testimonies of these women after years of being so manacled by my own shame. Little by little, I freed myself up as, night after night, I spoke, albeit in someone else's words, of the sadness, happiness, shame and sense of celebration women feel about their sexuality.

When *The Vagina Monologues* first opened in Dublin, it was a big deal. The box office got all sorts of strange calls, ranging from the pornographic to the religiously batty. The most common problem, though, was a result of the people who couldn't bring themselves to say the word 'vagina'.

The woman who ran the box office was nearing the end of her tether when a hapless lady rang looking to book tickets for the 'ehm monologues'.

'Forget about the mind,
the clitoris is a terrible thing to waste.'
Lisa Kogan

'Yes, there are some tickets left,' said the box office woman through gritted teeth.

'And . . . ehm . . . could you tell me please, what is the subject matter?' ventured the hapless lady.

There was a thinly disguised growl from the box office. 'Look, missus, it's called *The Vagina Monologues*. It's about the VAGINA! If it was about the thorax it would be called *The Thorax Monologues*. Now do you still want tickets?'

I don't think it was a show for the hapless.

7

Happiness

'The happiness of a person resides in one thing —
to be able to remain peacefully in a room.'
Blaise Pascal

Chasing a Hare

Two decades ago, during my third year with *Glenroe*, I found myself attending a tree-planting ceremony at a Buddhist conference. The trees symbolised the hope for the future, nature springing forth, and all that jazz. As the roots were going into the ground, I began to sob. The truth was, I didn't feel any hope for the future, not a glimmer. What I felt was completely at odds with my environment.

A friend who was beside me leaned over and whispered, 'Come off it, Mary, you are *such* an actress.' But I wasn't acting. This happened at a time when I had no understanding that I was depressed. My sadness was malignant and it attached itself to everything around me, to all the things I cared about. And I cared deeply about nature.

At around the same time, I went to see an alternative therapist to help me to relax through visualisation. She got me to lie down, close my eyes and bring myself to a state of inner quiet. Then she said in soothing tones, 'Imagine yourself sinking back into the earth. Feel the safety of the earth all around you, holding you and comforting you.'

But far from being guided into a relaxed state, I became

overwhelmed with sorrow. I stood up, crying. How could I imagine the earth holding me safely when the earth wasn't safe at all? Everybody was draining it of its resources, plundering it without any thought for the future.

This over-attachment to the wrongness of the world and lack of hope for the future have been ongoing symptoms of my depression. Yet, it might surprise you to know that I am not an unhappy person.

Unhappiness and depression are two different things. Of course they are intertwined, one informing the other, but at the same time, they are separate.

The longest period of happiness in my life was during my childhood. By happy, I mean ability to enjoy the present moment. All children, whether the general aura of their childhood is happy or not, can stay in a joyful moment – playing a game, letting their imagination run free, enjoying the company of friends – and, in that moment, they can achieve the nearest thing to what we adults perceive as happiness, for which we are on a constant search.

But as adults, life is more complex. Without a doubt, the years I spent working on *Glenroe* was a very happy era in my life. Yet, during it, I was suffering from depression. My dark days were tempered by my time on the set, where there was inevitably something to laugh about, or someone to make me crack up, no matter how bad I felt.

So, I was a depressed person and a happy person at the same time.

Life is dark and light. It's not perfect and it's not always fair. Unfortunately, every message given to us in advertisements and movies, magazine articles and love songs, sells a construct that there is this perfect life somewhere out there, probably being lived by someone else. We're taught to believe that happiness is a goal to pursue, something that can be finally achieved.

The pursuit of happiness is so ingrained in the collective consciousness that it has become one of our default settings. We pursue it automatically, and with that pursuit come stresses. It's like running after a hare you will never catch. You get sight of it every now and then, but just as you're about to pounce, it darts off in another direction and the chase begins again.

But happiness is not a hare that you have to chase with all your might. It is within your grasp already. It lies within you, resting in your own perceptions of the world.

When I was in my late teens, I read a book called *Testament of Youth* by Vera Brittain. Set during the First World War, it was her autobiography, describing how she lost her lover, her brother and many of the closest people in her life in the trenches, and how she forged ahead to make a career for herself in a society that didn't have much in the way of tolerance for educated women. In the book, Vera did not steer clear of her grief. Instead, she immersed herself in it. She felt it and found comfort in allowing herself to do so. Her grief was cathartic.

I think nowadays we are less able to deal with life in that sort of way. People were more modest back then because their expectations were limited. It is only since we have become wealthier in the West that we have grown to have this egoistic belief that life should always be good, that we should be able to control our fates and find ultimate happiness.

One of the few advantages of depression is that it lowers your expectations. You don't need huge, amazing things to make you happy. You're not always thinking *this* will make me happy, or *that* will make me happy. Sometimes you might be thinking you will never feel happiness again, but, then, when you least expect it, the light gets in through a crack and you really get to feel true joy.

Recently, I was out for a walk on the country lanes that surround my house and I bumped into a man I hadn't seen for a long time. We stood there, chatting in the early evening light and he told me about another person we both know who is ill, but had received very good news from the doctors that morning.

When I waved goodbye and went on my way, I felt suffused with happiness. It was a small thing, but it gave me joy. In reducing your expectations of what happiness is, or what will make you happy, depression automatically expands your capacity for happiness.

If I hadn't gone through depression, I would probably be rushing from the car into the house at night and I wouldn't look up at the stars and see how magnificent and beyond all comprehension the universe is. That would be two minutes of happiness down the Swanee straight away.

The Joy of Paris

In 1998, three years before I left *Glenroe*, I bought an apartment in Paris. It's on a tiny street called Rue de Savoie in the *plus posh* sixth arrondissement and it's no bigger than a shoebox.

I first visited the city in my early thirties, after *Glenroe* had been running for a couple of years. I was beginning to get attention on the street in Ireland and wasn't dealing with it very well. Parisians, however, had never heard of *Glenroe* or Biddy, and I felt a sense of freedom wandering the city's streets. I loved the lifestyle there, the beauty of the buildings, the cafés on every corner, the stylishness of the people, the way Paris wore itself like a subtly beautiful gown.

I began going to Paris regularly after that. Sitting at a table outside a café on the cobbles of Montparnasse, I didn't feel odd at all. I fitted right in. Even the way I dressed fitted in. In Paris, I could go to a bar by myself and sit with a glass of wine and a book and not be worried about how I was being perceived. There was a quiet freedom of self-expression in doing that, something I would never have allowed myself at home.

Parisians are not actively fashion conscious; they're more conscious of expressing their own personal style through their dress sense. On the street where my apartment is, I've seen some extraordinarily awfully dressed people and I've seen real originality and style. Parisians are all about finding their own personal look, and working that look to the best of their

'Paris is always a good idea.'
Audrey Hepburn

ability. I'm similar when it comes to fashion. I love clothes and I get great pleasure out of creating a look.

Picasso's famous mistress, Dora Marr, lived at Number 7, Rue de Savoie, a few doors from my place. I had been fascinated with her as a girl because she was so long-suffering of Picasso's moods and he called her his 'woman in tears'. The night he met her, she cut her fingers playing 'the knife game' on the table they were drinking at. Picasso took her blood-stained gloves home and added them to the collection of things he exhibited on the mantelpiece.

Dora was a wonderful photographer and painter in her own right too and I admired her work. I only discovered that she lived on the street after I bought the apartment and it seemed like a fitting coincidence. I also discovered that the building that houses my apartment was once part of Picasso's hotelier, where he painted *Guernica*.

You stick your head out one window of my apartment and you have a clear view of Notre Dame, stick your head out the other, and you see La Tour Montparnasse. One New Year's Day, Garvan and I watched the military flyover along the Champs-Élysées from our little window.

Buying the apartment meant owning a little piece of the city that was my sanctuary, a place I could always return to when I needed to let go and loosen up.

The city also had a freeing effect on my mother. After my father had died, I took her to Paris for a holiday and, one day over coffee, she began to share her memories of nursing in London during the Blitz. She told me of a bombing victim she had tended to, who had lost both his arms in the attack.

'Oh, that's horrible,' I said.

'Yes,' she replied. 'And the awful thing was that he was a gardener.' And then she broke down into tears.

It was a rare insight into the inner workings of my mother, and the pain she kept to herself throughout the years.

Today, I've spread my wings and have grown to love many other cities, but there will always remain a special place in my heart for Paris. Over the years, it has brought me great moments of that ever-elusive thing called happiness.

Leaving Glenroe

FOR SOMEBODY WHO HAS OFTEN FOUND HERSELF PARALYSED BY a fear of the future, it's ironic that I have always made the big decisions in my life very quickly.

I might have mused over leaving *Glenroe* during my last few years on the show, but I never really grappled with any decision about it. Then, one day I was on set and it just hit me: this is the day.

I loved *Glenroe* and I never wanted to say to myself, 'You

should have left it before it left you.' So, taking the bull by the horns, I went the very next morning and told the RTÉ bosses that I wanted to go. There was no weeping and gnashing of teeth – I suspect they were secretly delighted with my decision.

I didn't give up *Glenroe* because the series was coming to an end. I genuinely thought that they would round it off to 20 years with three more seasons. But, as it turned out, Biddy's death in a car crash (echoing my first day on set when I ran over the garda's motorcycle) was the beginning of *Glenroe's* goodbye.

In the end, my own goodbye to *Glenroe* was deeply painful. The last cast script reading, the last rehearsal period, the last location scene, the last studio scene . . . Each of these signalled another final step towards leaving my alternative family and the security I found with them for 16 incredibly formative years. But it had to be done.

It always surprises me how, bit by bit, we find the strength to do some things in life. I went through the process of leaving *Glenroe* one step at a time, almost like you do at the funeral of a loved one.

The series was axed during the following season, and I was much more upset when I heard that news than I was the day I left. As long as *Glenroe* was going on, there was a sort of Utopian idyll somewhere in the world for me.

Such was the level of interest in Biddy's demise that I ended up on the *Six One News* sharing my thoughts with the country about this shocking 'news' story. People came up to me in the street and told me they just couldn't believe it. Biddy was gone! It just went to show, you never knew what was coming around the corner.

When it didn't die down, the ongoing Biddy-curiosity began to get a bit too much for me. Everywhere I looked, it seemed someone had an opinion about it. I turned off all radios and televisions, and stopped buying papers for a while. I needed to let Biddy rest in peace in my own way, without the intrusion of media pundits.

Now that I was an ordinary member of the public, rather than an actor on a TV show, I was sure I would never get work again. I had been identified as a soap actress and everybody knew that once you were finished in a soap, you weren't employable as an actor again because the public identified you with your character too much. I needed to pay my way in the world, but I didn't really know how to do anything else except act, so I knew I would have gain another skill.

After examining my options, I figured that teaching English to foreign students was a good way forward. It would mean working with people who had never heard of me or of *Glenroe*, so I wouldn't have to explain constantly why I wasn't acting anymore. Although I had made the decision to leave RTÉ, I was embarrassed at my so-called loss of status.

I enrolled on a TEFL (Teaching English as a Foreign Language) course. Since leaving school over 20 years earlier I hadn't studied academically and I have to say I enjoyed every minute of the course. I loved learning and my fellow students were a fascinating bunch of travellers headed for the Far East and adventure. One was a wonderful woman who was learning to teach simply to fund her passion for dancing the tango.

As soon as I qualified, I got a job. I felt a small glow of satisfaction on my first day at my new place of work, a language school beside the sea in South County Dublin. I was happy that I could still earn my living and I relaxed into my new life, although I remained hopeful that the phone would ring with the offer of some exciting acting work.

I taught in the school for nine months. Summer arrived and with it a stretch of warm, balmy weather. Every day after work, I would trek down to the beach for a swim, where soon I became a regular, enjoying the good humour and banter of my fellow swimmers.

There was an atmosphere of lightness and acceptance on that beach that really opened my eyes. In a way, I had chosen to hide in the language school, from Biddy, from my former life, from the discomfort of not being a successful actor anymore. Yet day after day, I would go down to the beach, disrobe and go swimming with dozens of others who may have known my work on television, but didn't care who I was or what I had done. They had seen off lots of life's challenges and, in many cases, were still dealing with problems that would have completely defeated me.

They called the beach 'The Office' and every day they would gather to swim and chat and laugh at life's foibles. One late afternoon, as I was packing up my swimming things, I watched two elderly gentlemen gingerly make their way into the sea. It took them a while, but they eventually made it. As they acclimatised to the bracing temperature of the water, one of them let out a whoop and shouted to the other, 'Hey, Jem! Isn't it great to be young?' before they both swam off into the distance.

Years later, the memory of this makes me smile. They were a pair of teachers in the art of living.

On another of my afternoons in 'The Office', I was lying on a rock drying myself in the sun when my mobile rang. It was my agent. A very eminent theatre company wanted me to work for them. It was a good part, it would look well on my CV and would probably lead to more work with the company. In short, it was the wonderful opportunity I'd been secretly hoping for.

I should have been cartwheeling across the sand because of my good fortune, but instead I took a breath and told my agent that I would call her back.

All around me there were people of all ages shapes and sizes, women scarred from cancer, men crippled with arthritis, giddy teenagers and shrieking children. There were no perfect bodies, no 'beautiful people' posing, just a collection of ordinary, wounded, flawed human beings simply enjoying a summer's day by the sea.

I was suddenly overcome with affection for them, and deeply grateful that I was one of them. I rang my agent back and told her I wouldn't be taking the job. I just couldn't say goodbye to all this ordinary beauty.

To this day, I don't really know if I made the right decision. But I don't think it matters. I think I chose to be kind to myself and rather than successful. It felt better that way,

Turning the Poison into Medicine

UNLIKE MANY PEOPLE WHO ARE AFRAID OF EXPRESSING THE anger we all have inside, Mick Lally – my friend, on-screen husband in *Glenroe* and co-star in many theatrical productions thereafter – knew how to *be* angry. But his anger didn't get in the way of his happiness.

Instead of letting it fester, he let it flare. Sometimes, you might feel the brunt of it, and you might be hurt, but then the anger would be gone and no resentment would linger, on his part or anyone else's. His anger wasn't necessarily directed at you, it was just anger that needed expression and you might happen to be in the firing line. Once you understood that, you could get over it very quickly in the way you might be pelted by the hail in a storm, but the minute the clouds part you forget it. His anger was perfectly expressed.

I cannot express anger in that white-hot, pure way that Mick did. But I am learning. I admit that I have carried resentments of all kinds with me through my life, angers that I have nursed almost unknowingly through the years. But

*'When the Japanese mend broken objects, they aggrandise
the damage by filling the cracks with gold.
They believe when something has suffered damage
and has a history, it becomes more beautiful.'*
Barbara Bloom, American artist

resentment is anger turned inwards and it is utterly wasted. We affix blame and complain, yet do very little about our anger other than feel it. It fuels itself and grows to become a very negative force in our lives.

Depression is sometimes characterised as anger turned inwards, and I would say that although my resentments don't eat me up, they have underpinned my condition. They are not at the forefront of my life but they cheep-cheep away constantly inside, like day-old chicks. The fires of my resentment are stoked by all kinds of things, some personal, some reflecting the wider world. The ignorance of man, environmental decline and the failure of we humans to take responsible action to prevent it, racial, religious or sexual discrimination – all of these things can bed down in me to cause a sense of resentment. Other times, I am oversensitive to criticism and can harbour bad feeling, or I can take slight too easily and end up building resentment.

But in Buddhism, we learn to take responsibility for our own feelings, not to blame those outside ourselves for what is wrong with the world as we perceive it. You can still be angry – as long as you are turning the poison into medicine.

I once read an account written by a Buddhist woman who had been viciously raped. During her ordeal, she had begun to chant. Then, her assailant began to chant too – he mocked her prayers while he violated her.

Now your perception of Buddhists might be that we are a crowd of airheads floating around on little fluffy clouds, always at the ready to forgive and forget and chalk it down to spiritual experience. But did this woman forgive her mocking rapist? Like hell, she did. Her chant while he was raping her was, 'I am not going to be a victim. I am not going to be a victim.'

In the aftermath of her ordeal, she reported her rapist, took him to court and won her case. She used her anger to get justice in her life. She was saying, 'I am precious. I am a child of the universe and I have as much right to be here as the moon and the stars. *You do not violate me.*'

She explained that she didn't carry her anger with her once she had seen justice done for herself. I believe this was because she had used her anger correctly. It didn't turn inward, it went out. She let her rapist know he couldn't violate her, that he couldn't do it to anyone.

Violent rape may be an extreme example, but I think it is important to put the lesson of expressing anger in its right form into practice in our everyday existence. Anger has a place and purpose in life. We all have it and we all have the need and the right to express it at certain times, some more than others. I call it 'compassionate anger'. And it can fuel change, rather than fuel itself.

When you're feeling angry at the injustices in life, or at your neighbour, or at your parents, friends, brother or sister, or at your government, it's a good idea to keep that phrase in mind: go on, give a lot. Take the energy created by your anger and put it to good use. Turn the poison into medicine. Because if you don't, and take action rooted in resentment instead, you are setting yourself up for negative consequences down the line. Similarly, if you act out of a sense of revenge, you will the one left dealing with the bad effects.

Awareness of this cause and effect helps me deal with my anger. It makes me step back. I go to my altar to chant and the effect is like washing the problem – suddenly it either goes away or I see a clearer way of dealing with it. The poison gets turned into medicine.

Getting Off the Merry-Go-Round

STATISTICS SHOW THAT DEPRESSION IS ON THE RISE. HOW COULD this be? Society is more open now than ever before. People have more choices in life. There is more information and knowledge available to us than ever before. Children are more loved, childhood is more valued, and we all have a lot more understanding of the difficulties experienced through adolescence.

For all of that, in the Western world at least, there seem to be more people who are unhappy than ever before. Wealth and consumerism cannot fix one key problem: the frailty of the human condition.

As humans, we are vulnerable creatures. It can be easy to forget in day-to-day living, but it takes very little to break us. Each of us is imperfect. None of us is invincible. We all grow old. We all die. Yet we have created a society that worships at the altar of youth, strength and achievement. Somehow we creatures who, by our very nature, are vulnerable, have created a world that eschews weakness of any kind.

We are under constant sensory bombardment from newspapers, magazines, television, billboards, video games and the internet, enticing us with cocktails of unattainable perfection and success.

I don't blame the media. The media has existed since Adam was a boy and it has a perfect right to speak as it finds. Unfortunately, it has grown to become a vast entity that places unseen borders on our lives, convincing us that we should be a certain way, that life should be a certain way, that the world should be a certain way.

As I write this, out of the corner of my eye, I can see the cover of one of my magazines, featuring an airbrushed Gwyneth Paltrow who promises to tell me all about 'fame, fashion and family', as if fame and fashion came anywhere near the importance of family. The biggest headline on the page shouts: 'Your 2011 Guide To Gorgeous', highlighting a feature that's going to give me lots of tips about how to be a perfect specimen of female humanity this year.

Like many others, I love indulging in these magazines. They call out like sirens from the shelves of newsagent shops, beseeching me to buy them, and I do. I love taking them home and flicking through them, savouring the images of thin, gorgeous models, reading about the happy lives of the beautiful and how, if I spend some money, I might attain such happiness in my own life.

I'm aware that I am an impressionable soul. I might pretend that I'm not influenced by such easy-to-consume drivel, but I am, just as much as the next person. Sometimes, it feels like the media message of attainable perfection is so all-pervasive that it's impossible to step back, evaluate and discern. To do so, you need to have a strong sense of self, and you need to keep your feet on the ground and centre yourself. For those of us who struggle with depression, these qualities aren't always the easiest to come by.

I don't believe, however, that it's just depressed people who feel discontented and destabilised by the emphasis on overachievement the media brings with it. To a great extent, we have ditched religion and chosen to be more autonomous, but we have substituted it with consumerism. Now the capitalist economy is the altar we kneel at. The capitalist God needs to be fed, so we are compelled to buy stuff and lots of it. Naturally it's in a lot of people's interest to try and sell us that stuff, and we collude with enthusiasm, like lambs to the slaughter.

It's a merry-go-round that's hard to get off. If I could just

'Wonder will never be lacking in the world.
What is lacking is wonderment.'
G. K. Chesterton

have this, I'll be happy. If I looked like that, I'd be happy. If I wore those clothes, I'd be happy. If I went on that holiday, I'd be happy. But those wheels never stop turning. Enough is never enough.

For me, yoga is a mechanism through which I can slow down. It's about going within rather than looking without, moving under all the layers of anxiety and calming the mind. It's about stepping off the merry-go-round.

The great thing about doing yoga is that you can become the observer of your thoughts, rather than be enslaved by them.

Happiness, therefore, is a strange combination of both lowering your expectations and expanding them at the same time. If your idea of happiness is being able to go and spend €500 in Dundrum Shopping Centre, that's fine. But remember that it will only make you happy for the half hour you're spending. If you're anything like me, you're going to come home and feel a bit guilty about spending the money, and maybe worried about your bank balance too.

Getting to a place of stillness and peace, feeling centred in yourself in one moment, is enough to make you happy. It is, in fact, the essence of happiness.

In doing that simple thing – for me it's yoga, but for you it might be as simple as making a cup of tea and sitting quietly in the back garden with it once the children are in bed – you expand your expectations. You become connected to a greater sense of yourself, to a vast universe of true, not manufactured, happiness.

In a similar way that buying things does not bring happiness, other people do not assure it either. This is a lesson that people who suffer from depression can find difficult to learn. We do not feel we have the strength to make ourselves happy, so we may reach out and make our happiness depend upon the behaviour of other people.

Trying to control other people's behaviour is as futile as trying to stop ice from melting under the summer sun. Sooner or later, people will do something that won't wash well with you, something that, if you are not careful, you will turn into a misguided reason for your unhappiness.

If you can't find happiness sitting by yourself in your own space, you will never find it anywhere else.

It only takes a little effort and then you can get back up on the merry-go-round safe, in the knowledge that when you want to step off again, you can.

Hope Floats

I KNOW THAT, IN MY INTRODUCTION, I TALKED ABOUT HOPING being a passive state of mind and not great for creating a better future, but I do believe that for a happy life, you have to live in hope too.

So here are my own hopes for myself.

Today I am going for lunch with Garvan. I hope that we have lovely food and a good chat. This is a 'least you can do' hope, and it is enough to get me looking forward with happiness in this moment. If there is somebody who needs help today, I hope I can help then in some real way, for the sake of it.

On a grander scale, I hope not to have to take anti-depressants into the future, but it's not the biggest hope I have. If they are part of my life until the end of my life, so be it. I can accept that.

I hope to make enough money to develop the farmland I inherited from my parents further. I would love to experiment with keeping animals and making a living from them without them having to be slaughtered.

I hope to keep on examining life, to continue having moments of great clarity about existence.

I hope to run the marathon when I am 60.

I hope to be an actress who contributes to a positive statement about older women.

I hope to get more donkeys. Three are just not enough in my book.

I hope to stay really healthy into active into old age. I want my old age to be my crowning glory.

I hope that people will realise that the earth we stand on

has given us everything we have and everything we are, and it deserves our love, respect and care in return.

I hope that George Clooney will stop hanging around with skinny young ones half his age and realise that a sturdy Westmeath woman with a farm behind her is a far better bet.

I hope to continue on my wonderful, painful and joyful journey through life.

8

❧ Ageing ❧

'None are so old as those who have outlived enthusiasm.'
Henry David Thoreau

The Ginger Man

THE FIRST PLAY I AGREED TO DO AFTER LEAVING *GLENROE* WAS J.P.
Donleavy's wonderful *The Ginger Man*. Set in Dublin in the
1950s, it explores repressed Irish sexuality as its Irish-American
hero Sebastian Dangerfield encounters life as a Trinity student.
I played Miss Frost, a shy and retiring lodger who lived with
Dangerfield and his wife. It was a small part, and I thoroughly
enjoyed it. The play was such a success during its Dublin run,
that it was picked up for a tour of Wales and on to New York.
It was an exciting time, even if it was tempered by difficulties
at home.

The moment when the first inkling of my mother's
dementia became clear will be imprinted on my own memory
for ever. We were driving together into Delvin to visit her best
friend and suddenly she couldn't remember where her friend
lived. She became confused and upset.

After that, the dementia slowly took hold. Thank God it
never got to to the level where she was so confused that she
wasn't able to function. She remained living at home and she
could look after herself, but her short-term memory became

so bad that if you had a conversation with her, five minutes later she wouldn't remember it.

Mum didn't know who had died or who was still alive. Every day for her was like Groundhog Day and what made it worse was that she was fully aware of her loss of memory. It was hard to see someone like her, who was such a disciplined and strong woman, fading in this way.

I employed a family friend, a woman called Keum Jok, to look after Mum while I was working. But just before *The Ginger Man* was about to set sail for America, Keum's own mother died suddenly and she had to fly home to Malaysia. Lucky for me, Mum had great neighbours, particularly her friend Pauline, who stepped in while I was away with the play and looked after her until Keum came back.

The Ginger Man was in a theatre so far 'off Broadway', it was practically on the Aran Islands. A huge part of my mind was still at home with my mother, but boy did I love New York! It was brash, noisy and dirty, but packed to the brim with life and possibility. Everybody there seemed to be the star of their own private movie.

We were a small production, so it was all hands on deck. By day, the cast did all the flyering and postering across the city for the play. One afternoon, I was out putting up posters in Irish pubs on the West Side. I was starving, so I nipped into a pizza joint. I barked my order, got the pizza and, while wolfing it down, planned my trip 'cross town' to Lexington Avenue to do more postering. I suddenly stopped and thought, 'Sheesh!

Here I am. Mary Mac from the bog, ducking and weaving in the Big Apple!' It was a great moment.

Everyone knows the famous line from the song 'New York New York' – 'If I can make it there, I'll make it anywhere' – but for me it was more about surviving there, rather than 'making it'. In that moment, I knew that I could and the feeling of my own strength was thrilling.

It is moments like these that I celebrate and cherish. The attention and (if you are lucky) praise that you get in showbiz is nice, but it is also fickle and fleeting. It's the moments of attention and praise you give yourself that mean something and that last. That moment in New York what I felt was more precious than any good review. It was a feeling of satisfaction in the here and now.

I didn't have to bring Broadway to a standstill with the brilliance of my performance to feel happy. I just had to get that crosstown bus.

The Change of Life

DESPITE MY DIRE PREDICTIONS THAT I WOULD NEVER ACT AGAIN after *Glenroe*, I ended up working more than I ever had in the past. A period began where Mick and I were very popular as a double act on the theatrical circuit, first in *The Chastitute* and then *The Field*, both by John B. Keane.

HOW THE LIGHT GETS IN

'Knowledge comes, but wisdom lingers.'
Alfred, Lord Tennyson

During one 10-month tour of the country with *The Field*, things started to get too much. Mum was going further and further downhill and, to top it off, I began to go through the menopause earlier than is usual. I was suffering from all sorts of hormonal ups and downs, marked by terrible fits of anxiety.

We had Sundays off from the show and I would travel home from wherever we were after the Saturday night performance, no matter what the distance. While I was home, I'd do the cooking for the week and put it in the deep freeze, while trying to chat to my mother and be there for her. It was a difficult time, and I was getting increasingly exhausted, having to manage it all.

We fought a lot. I was so tired and hormonal that I didn't have the patience to deal the constant questions that came with her state of mind. She forgot every answer I gave her within a few minutes and then would ask the same question again. Before too long, I was living in a state of constant anxiety, completely strung out. Every single little *i* had to be dotted, every *t* crossed. I was obsessing about the tiniest little thing and not able to sleep at night for worrying.

By now Mum's previous carer had moved on, and a series of new carers managed her during the week. And they were fantastic. I knew she was in good hands, but, at the same time, in the depths of my anxiety, I couldn't let go.

It was a vicious circle. I had to keep working to keep my mum cared for. I thought about stopping and taking care of her myself, but that wouldn't have suited either of us. We had become so alike as we had got older, and we clashed constantly. That might have been all right when the two of us were younger women, but not now – neither of us were able for it anymore and, besides, who would want to be left with a sense of regret that you couldn't live out your last years together in peace?

I wish I'd had more patience with Mum then, and I am sure that if it was the other way round, she would wish she could have had more patience with me. But we muddled through. One of the positive upshots of Mum's short-term memory was that, if we did have a row, she wouldn't remember it five minutes later. And we always ended up having a cup of tea. I would apologise for being impatient with her, and she'd say it was okay.

I did some work for The Carers' Association a few years back and I found that carers have the blackest sense of humour. They recognise the reality that, unless you have the patience of Mother Teresa, there are times when you do get frustrated or annoyed, and there is nothing you can do about it. They also recognise the love that you have for the person you are caring for.

The only way I could tell Mum that I loved her was in writing. So every card I gave her, on her birthday, Mother's Day and Christmas, all contained the words, 'I love you,

Mum'. I've kept those cards and look at them from time to time to remind myself that I did my best.

Coping with her memory loss and my menopause at the same time was often overwhelming. For many depression sufferers, the hormonal rollercoaster that is menopause only adds to their symptoms. I was beyond myself with anxiety and that malignant sadness had seeped deep into my bones.

I didn't mind my periods stopping, but I hated the weight gain. I hated the matronly way I started to look, but, mostly, it was the mental pain that ground me down. I didn't have many physical symptoms at all. Hot flushes come and go, but my anxiety was outrageous and constant.

I had no regrets whatsoever about it being the end of my childbearing years – in fact, I was glad that I could now have sex without worrying about getting pregnant. But hitting the menopause was undeniable proof that I was getting older and that was where my difficulties lay. There was a sense of shame about not being in the thick of life any more. For a time, I felt sorrowful about this. But that has started to change. Recently, I have begun to see things anew. Coming through menopause has granted me a fresh start. I recognise how far I have come, and have much farther I have to go. I prefer the person I am now to the one I was before the menopause.

Middle age grants us with an opportunity to stand our ground and refuse to conform to the expectations of others. Life experience has given us something valuable to say, and not just to our own age group.

We watch nature programmes that tell us every little shift in the balance is part of the greater pattern. Human beings are no different in that way from the animals portrayed in David Attenborough's *Life on Earth*. There is a forward-motion purpose to everything in natural life, and the menopause is part of our personal evolution rather than our decline.

When all is said and done, it can be a passage to power because there is nothing to lose anymore. The cranky old woman is a stereotype that society has created to take that power away, but if we could harness that power, it becomes a great thing, for everyone.

The Invisible Women

A FEW YEARS AGO SOME OF US GLENROVIANS WERE INVITED TO the *TV Now* Awards. We were delighted to be asked and we girls had great fun getting 'red-carpet ready', even if we felt a bit daunted by all the shenanigans. All this glamour was relatively new to the Irish showbiz scene – it certainly hadn't been a feature in our day.

Looking immaculate, we tottered down to the awards venue in our car-to-bar shoes and frilly frocks. There was a wall of photographers flanking either end of the red carpet beside the door. 'Here we go, Mary,' I whispered to myself, sucking in my stomach and preparing for my moment in the camera-flash sun.

Just as our high heels were about to land on the carpet, a young lassie from *Emmerdale* arrived, wearing a lime green belt that passed for a dress. The paparazzi all turned in her direction like a battery of Daleks and proceeded to click like crazy as she posed for them prettily.

The *Glenroe* girls and I stood there, not knowing what to do until a very nice hostess suggested we go inside. We scuttled in, ducking behind Michelle Heaton, who had replaced Emmerdale Girl for the photographers' attentions.

Truth be told, we all found the whole episode very funny. We had no illusions. In a world that trades on youthful glamour, we were more *TV Then* than *TV Now*.

To the young, age seems such a long way off. When I was 20, middle age was located somewhere in the distant mists of time. Now I am middle-aged, post-menopausal and looking back instead of forward, time has concertinaed and my twenties seem like last year. My body has changed but my mind has, if anything, become more eager for life. I think I'm a stronger person, a wiser person and, in my professional life, I would hope, a better actress for it.

Often when I get together with my friends, we end up talking about our experience of ageing. We sit there in a slightly bemused state, asking ourselves how and when did this happen? On the whole we are quite happy with our lot and most of us would choose not to be young again. However there is one aspect of ageing that all of us find frustrating – our growing invisibility. Having to adjust to the changing reality of ageing – that whatever chance you ever had of being the girl in the lime green dress, is long gone now – isn't always easy.

When I was a young woman, because of the success of *Glenroe*, everyone seemed to want my opinion on everything. I was asked to do advertising campaigns and I got invited to speak at openings and launches regularly. All this attention was heaped upon me despite the fact that I didn't know my arse from my elbow.

Admittedly, working in television automatically made me more visible, but, looking back, I think it was my youth that really drew the attention. I still consistently work as an actress and still appear regularly on television, but I'm no longer young, so when I go to functions, I find myself unnoticed at the edges of the room, while the young and glossy take centre stage.

While the invisibility of age can be very restful, it has a dangerous side. When we disappear from the stage, not only are we not seen, but we cease to matter. The movers and shakers of the world are increasingly young and the opinions and rights of the middle- and old-aged are overlooked. The general opinion would appear to be that we've had our turn. We should go away and do whatever the old do – mow the lawn, knit, drink Complan and die without causing too much trouble.

On the streets there are no billboards featuring good-looking senior citizens. There are no middle-aged cover girls. The only things deemed worth selling to us are stairlifts, TENA Lady and life insurance, so our nearest and dearest won't have to fork out to bury us. Ever heard of Keith Richards, Patti Smith, Jack Nicholson or Iggy Pop? There are millions of grey-haired delinquents who know just as much about rule-breaking and adventure now as they did in their twenties.

Depression reappeared for me during the menopause, when I finally realised that I was middle-aged. For the first time in my life, I felt that I had something of value to say, but now no one wanted to hear it.

To add to that, although I was slowly but surely growing to accept how I looked and appreciate my appearance and healthy body, I found myself running into a brick wall of judgement and preconceptions because I – shock, horror! – had physically aged.

It's the twenty-first century. Everywhere we look the message is reflected: you can get older, but you sure as hell better not start *looking* older.

The Madonna Complex

BACK WHEN I WAS IN MY THIRTIES AND HAD THE PRIVILEGE OF working with Siobhán McKenna in *Bailegangaire*, we shared a dressing room. I loved watching Siobhán doing her make-up for the performance. I would sit enraptured as she painted her face, a little here, a little there, preparing herself to stand in front of her audience.

She was well into her sixties by then, with pale, Celtic skin that had its fair share of wrinkles, but I was always struck by her beauty. It was not just the character and wisdom in her ageing face – to me she was more physically beautiful than any photographs I had seen of her in her youth. Her age had added soul to her beauty, making it far more striking.

Actresses like Siobhán McKenna, valued for the fine depth that age adds to their features, are few and far between nowadays. Instead we have mega-celebrities like Madonna who are valued for never appearing to age.

A part of me has always liked Madonna, though, because she refuses to be shamed, either physically or sexually, despite constantly being told to 'put it away' and be age appropriate.

Why should she? I love the fact that she presents her generation of women with an alternative image to that of the matron. Fair enough, her levels of fitness are almost super human and being rich as Cresus certainly helps in the search for eternal hotness, but I believe the image she projects of a vital, physically fit and sexual woman in her fifties is important.

At the same time, the articles in *Heat* magazine, exposing Madonna's 'old lady' hands, belie the fact that in every image sold to us by the queen of pop, she looks unbelievably young for her age. The images we see of her are manipulated to the point that we don't really know what she looks like at all, and *we're* being manipulated to believe that women in their fifties can look like wrinkle-free women in their early thirties: the lie that perfection and eternal youth are achievable.

Who Madonna really is is anyone's guess, as she exists in a polarity of media stereotype. There is no in-between – either you look horrifically and shamefully old or you look amazingly young for your age.

This lack of in-between is a dangerous prospect. Today, it is perfectly normal for an older actress or singer to come on to a TV chat show with a half-paralysed face. It is not unusual to go to a film in which an actress (rarely the actor) goes through a whole range of emotions, from fear to sadness, joy to rage, without ever registering it through her facial expressions.

It has become so acceptable for people to inject botulism into their foreheads, pump collagen into their lips and filler into their cheeks to look younger, that nobody even remarks on it. The trout pout has become a fact of life. Foreheads so smooth you could land a small aircraft on them are par for the course.

I can understand why people go for plastic surgery. It's a way of trying to ensure they are not swept away in the ever-rising tide of youth culture, an effort to stave off becoming invisible.

Personally, I would never have a facelift and Botox is out of the question. I want my face to look like a face. With few exceptions, as far as I'm concerned, all Botox or plastic surgery do is make people appear desperate. They are colluding with the prevailing lie that youth is the only desirable thing about life. When I see women who get these skin plumping treatments resulting in the infamous pillow face, I think of Siobhán McKenna's truly beautiful, aged face and wonder, 'What's the point of it all?'

The French have a better perspective on ageing. They see it as a refining process rather than one of diminishment. I'm a big fan of French films. In any one of them, there will be a woman who is over 50: it's the norm. She can be the romantic lead, she can be the seductress: she can be anything she wants to be. She's not a cougar, she is not a baby snatcher – she is just an attractive woman and her age is immaterial.

In Praise of Older Women

I WAS IN A SHOP THE OTHER DAY, LOOKING FOR A GREETING CARD. On the stand, I found a birthday card featuring a group of middle-aged ladies. The caption read: 'You know you are old when all your friends smell of piss.'

What kind of world do we live in, where ageing is portrayed as a disgusting joke and that's A-okay? Comedians can say awful things about older people, things they wouldn't dare say about black, Jewish or gay people. Apart from anything else, they know they'd be lynched. Why is it absolutely acceptable to make fun of older people?

My parents were elderly for a large part of my life, and I have huge respect for older people. I see the power and honour of ageing, rather than the diminishing idea of slipping into so-called dotage.

A society that enjoys a card like the one I found in that shop has to ask some searching questions of itself. Of its rejection of the ageing process, despite the fact that if we are lucky enough, each and every member of that society will get old.

I watched a documentary about the American founders of feminism recently. A fair few of them now live by themselves in cottages in the woods. They all remained very articulate and radical in their opinions. One of them in particular made absolutely not one scrap of effort to beautify herself. Her intellect was everything to her, that was all she cared about projecting. There she was, a woman full of life experience, living on her own in the woods and espousing views that didn't fit in with the patriarchy, at ease with her natural, aged appearance. In the Middle Ages, she might have been burned as a witch for not toeing the line.

Gaining invaluable experience as we live through good and bad, and growing in our understanding about the nature of life, are the true gains of growing older, something that should not only be celebrated, but appreciated and listened to for the good of us all.

It's natural to struggle with the physical changes that come with ageing. I look in the mirror some mornings and say to myself, 'Jesus, Mary and Joseph, look at those wrinkles. They weren't there yesterday, were they?' There's no doubt it's a challenging process, but we need to balance acceptance and understanding of the value of ageing, and take the appropriate steps to stay as healthy and vital as we can.

Ageing is not something that we can avoid, but neither do we have to age before our time. We can make the most of diet and exercise to stay active for much longer. Today, the potential life span for a healthy life is longer than ever before.

Getting older is what you make it. I don't see any reason not to go swimming in the lake in my wet suit. I don't see any reason not to try and run a marathon. I don't see any reason not to mess around like a teenager. I don't see any reason not to dance at a gig at the foot of the stage. Just because I'm older and have more experience doesn't mean I can't shake my booty with the best of them.

When we age, we have some understanding of youth, because we were once young ourselves. When we're young, naturally we don't have any desire to think about ageing. And it's easier to disregard what you don't understand. When age is disregarded, the world becomes a less caring place in which to age or be sick. The old and vulnerable become a costly inconvenience.

To me, one of the saddest things is an old person who is lonely and isolated. To have lived and loved, worked and adventured, and then to find yourself alone and disregarded at the end of your life is surely a worse fate than living fast and dying young.

The onus is upon older people to choose to live our lives in communication with the young. If we choose to fade into the background and become invisible, we are relinquishing the right to influence younger people, and growing old, something that happens to each and every one of us, will for ever be seen as a negative.

The Power of Kindness

I WOULD LIKE TO TELL YOU THE STORY OF A TRUE SPORTING HERO. I don't even know this hero's name but I had the privilege of seeing him run in the men's Leinster 400-metre final of the Special Olympics about 15 years ago.

I have never forgotten him. Life had handed him many challenges, and he was the only competitor in the race. His only objective was to get around the course. About halfway round, he got into difficulties and it looked like he wasn't going to make it. The crowd had been cheering him on, but when we saw him falter we got to our feet as one and started to roar our encouragement.

He picked himself up and battled on right to the finishing line, where he fell into the arms of a waiting supporter. The crowd went crazy – it was like a cup final. It was one of the most inspiring things I've ever seen, both the moment on the finishing line and the crowd's action and reaction.

There was no status, fame, endorsements or big cheques involved in this sporting moment. There was only one runner on the track, but it was a hugely exciting race that caused a very large group of people to rise in unison and urge a fellow human being to reach his goal, just for the joy of seeing him do it. The occasion not only showed the true meaning of sport, but the power of kindness. And the crowd received as much as they gave.

In today's cut-and-thrust world, movers and shakers are admired and rewarded, but a society that overvalues certain attributes is in danger of neglecting others. Kindness is not about the cut and thrust and it has nothing to do with instant self-gain or efficiency. The realities around age, vulnerability and sickness don't always sit comfortably with the egotistical march of progress.

When was the last time you heard of someone who had a blinding flash of true joy while taking 10 meetings a day? Did anyone ever feel the wonderful freedom that comes with being non-judgemental while doing spreadsheets? Did any child ever say they felt really happy because his parents were so busy?

We push ourselves hard to reach some notion of future perfection. We look up to those we perceive as being perfect, doggedly wanting the same for ourselves. But what have these people actually achieved?

Let's look at the world of sport again, an arena where the pursuit of perfection is paramount. Athletes, both professional and amateur, strive to achieve levels of fitness that, given the amounts of performance-enhancing drugs that are available, are humanly impossible. I'm always mystified as to why a person would rejoice in a victory that has been achieved by taking drugs. How can lying about your perfection be in the slightest bit satisfying?

The desire for challenge, venturing forth into the unknown and self-improvement are innate to humanity, and are wonderful things. But these concepts differ from person to person. If we emphasise self-advancement to the extent that the bigger picture becomes eclipsed, we can unknowingly sacrifice much of the beauty of life.

Kindness won't win you a promotion in your job or get you awards or medals. It doesn't require you to be brittle and witty or the fastest runner in the race. Kindness is everyday ordinariness in action, and it is one of life's greatest gifts, available to each and every one of us. When we are not afraid to be ordinary, to recognise that there is more to life than winning at all costs, it's possible for us to blossom in a way that is authentic. Ordinary kindness enables us to shine in a gentler way.

We need to be kinder to older people, not only in the way we treat them, but also in the way we think of them. We need to tap into the energy of that crowd cheering on the athlete whose goal is to make the finishing line, reflecting back the perfection in our humanity just as we are, celebrating the fact that we've got this far and honouring the life we have led to get here. The more Botox we inject, the more airbrushing of the truth about ageing we do. And the more we deride age as something to be shunned, the less opportunity we create to value its gifts, and treat it with the respect and kindness it deserves.

The more I age, the more I realise just how fleeting this stay on earth is, in the grand scheme of things. Living with kindness as a guiding virtue is an opportunity to maximise on the gifts that age brings: wisdom, dignity, time to consider, and the chance to hand down what we've learned to the next generation before our time is up.

9

Death

'A deathbed is such a special and sacred place:
a deathbed is more an altar than a bed.
It is an altar where the flesh and blood of a life
is transformed into eternal spirit.'
John O'Donoghue, *Divine Beauty*

The Little Red Hen

ON 29 SEPTEMBER 2003, MY MOTHER WAVED ME OFF AT THE DOOR as I drove back to Dublin for rehearsals of Willie Russell's *Shirley Valentine*. She was dressed and ready to go in the jeep to count the cattle with our good friend, Tommy, as she did every morning. It was a sunny day and she looked healthy and happy, smiling as she said goodbye.

The next morning at 9 a.m., my phone rang. It was Angela, Mum's carer. Hearing the news that followed, I felt as though I'd been thumped in the chest. Mum had died suddenly from a heart attack.

I've always been interested in the notion from old lore that the dying pick who they will die in front of. Some people choose to die alone, others not to. Mum was with her carers Molly and Angela when she died, and that's exactly what she would have wanted. I believe she would have wanted to spare me.

After the phone call, I was in that daze of shock and grief that comes with such sudden news. It seemed unreal, yet it was all too real. But how could Mum be gone? Garvan drove me to Delvin and my wonderful neighbours and friends gathered round. Their love and support carried me through the days to come.

There is a strange grace that emerges around death, a kind of sacredness. I experienced it with the death of both of my parents. There are huge lessons to be learned from the experience, not the least of which is the humility and the understanding of human kindness. We are all humble in the face of death's inevitability. And the human kindness that surrounded me in those difficult days was something to behold, and was in itself humbling.

As we did with Dad, we waked Mum in the house. Her friends and neighbours stayed up with me all night and a candle burned in the hall where she was laid out.

When she was in the midst of her dementia, Mum had a fixation about her hens. She loved those birds and would be in and out and in and out the henhouse 10 times a day to check that their eggs were all right, making sure the magpies didn't get them. The hens, on the other hand, were far too stuck up to come near the house, keeping strictly to their own territory.

The evening of Mum's wake, with the house full, I went out into the hall and found a little red hen standing beside her coffin, clucking quietly, not at all perturbed by the number of people milling around.

Buddhists say that the essence of the soul doesn't leave

the body for many hours after a person dies. I think the hen came into the house because the essence of Mum was still with us. The hen had come to say goodbye.

Everyone laughed out loud as the hen finally made her way out through the kitchen to the back door. We do funerals really well in Ireland because we know the value of not being embarrassed about braying with laughter about something when there is a corpse right beside you. Death is not sanitised here, it's a vital part of life.

Mum was buried on the anniversary of my father's death on a similarly glorious, sunny September's day. When her coffin was carried out of the house, everybody said it was like a queen leaving her castle. Her bridge club formed a guard of honour. My Aunt Eileen and I walked behind the coffin, Mum's last remaining relatives. I remember that as one of the hardest moments.

I have a friend who was a carer to her mother much in the same way as I was before Mum died. After her own mother's recent death, she felt overcome by the deep need to sleep, so that's exactly what she did. She slept a lot and waited until the next step became clear.

I think this is a good way to deal with grief. Sometimes my friend is happy, sometimes she's sad, sometimes she feels lost, and sometimes she feels angry. She respects each mood and gives it its space, all the while getting on with the day-to-day living of her life. She's not trying to jump to the next phase of grief or get it over with because it's painful and uncomfortable.

As the eminently wise John B. Keane once wrote: 'Calm yourself and be content to wait.'

I miss my mother. I can't pretend that our relationship was straightforward – or that I didn't always hold out the hope that we could make something better. But we loved each other and, as time went on, came to accept each other for who we were. And at the end of the day, who can really ask more of another person, regardless of your differences.

About three days after she had died, I sat in the kitchen with Garvan and Tommy, who had helped her count the sheep. I thought back to all those years ago, when the unit of three was me, Mum and Dad, united against the world. I needed to be alone in that space, to symbolically become my own unit, without my parents. Garvan and Tommy kindly gave me that space, and I sat by myself for a while, pensive and comfortable. That night I stayed in the house by myself for the first time ever. It wasn't lonely, it wasn't frightening – it felt absolutely right. The next day, I made my decision to move home to the farm for good.

'A man's dying is more the survivor's
affair than his own.'
Thomas Mann

Life Goes On

IN BUDDHISM, LIFE IS NOT LINEAR: BIRTH AND DEATH AREN'T THE beginning and end. The past, present and future are all one.

When friends of mine lose their parents or loved ones, I always say, 'In my experience, the relationship goes on.' It's my firm belief. Although Mum is no longer alive, I have a comforting feeling of her presence in the house with me at odd times. Dad comes too, whenever he takes the notion.

Some essence of them remains with me, and part of me is with them. I don't go to visit their grave very often because their home is where they are, on the farm and in the house with me.

I'm not Mystic Meg. It's not like I sit around with cards or Ouija boards trying to communicate with the hidden realm, and I wouldn't describe my experiences of feeling my parents' presence as clairvoyant. It's more everyday and mundane than that. Sometimes it's even funny.

The day of my father's funeral, for instance, Mum and I went out to lunch with my aunt and a few of my cousins. At the lunch we ordered a bottle of white and two glasses of red wine. Before I could take a sip of my glass of red, I accidentally spilled it all over the pristine white tablecloth. Next my cousin knocked her glass over. The bottle of white wine was in a cooler beside the table. My other cousin's elbow hit the cooler and the whole thing went flying. Every drop of wine we ordered had been spilled. I'm sure the waiter thought we were plastered before we even arrived.

Daddy had loathed alcohol. He had never taken a drink in his life and although he would always buy someone a drink, he didn't like people going to the pub or getting drunk.

I just shrugged and laughed, 'Well, thanks a lot, Dad, but you're not running the show in this realm,' and I ordered another bottle of wine.

If my father asserted his moral code after his funeral, after her death my mother made her presence felt in a different way. She came to give solace.

A few months after I moved back to the farm, I was praying at my altar. As I chanted, I looked at a small, framed photograph of her silhouetted against a sunset. It was a dull day and, in the afternoon gloom, Mum's face was hardly visible. I became overwhelmed with grief, bent in two and crying from the pit of my stomach. When I looked up again, a prick of sunlight had come through the clouds outside and was illuminating the photograph. Every feature on her face became clear and I let my grief lift.

All her life, Mum had been a great lover of the Queen. If anything was on television about the British royalty, we'd have to all sit down quietly and watch it. Dad and I would be rolling our eyes to heaven, muttering, 'the feckin' Queen' to each other, but Mum wouldn't even see us, she would be so enthralled.

A year ago, the BBC showed a four-part docu-drama about

Queen Elizabeth II's life and times. Different episodes were played by different actresses, all of whom I admired, so I found myself rushing home every Monday evening to catch it. One evening, while cuddled up on the couch in front of the telly, the significance struck me. Here I was, a person who had never been in the least interested in the Queen, and had always been at best bemused by my mother's interest, absolutely transported by a programme about her life and times. The hairs on the back of my neck rose up. At that moment, I knew that Mum was there with me, fully present. I chose that moment to make my peace with her.

'Mum,' I said aloud, 'I'm so sorry that I ever hurt you intentionally or unintentionally. You know I really love you.' I felt she got my message and, at that moment, something inside me came to rest.

In Buddhism, there's a Japanese word 'shi-me', which, roughly translated, means 'mission', but it also means 'to use life'. There is also the belief that we choose our parents for each life we live. I sometimes think that it was my mission to be with my parents in their lifetime. Now that mission has been completed, beyond the grief, I experience a new sense of freedom. Although I grieved hugely and I still have moments of absolute sadness at their passing, at the same time I'm glad I have the space and freedom to develop now. I'm doing work on myself that another woman coming from a different set of circumstances might have done in her twenties.

When my parents were alive, I always worried about what

their reaction would be before I did anything, and to some
extent this would inform my choice. I'm a lot more vocal
these days than I would have been seven years ago, before my
mother died. I feel I can step out now and truly be myself.

Snowball

TWO YEARS AGO, I DID THE REGIONAL TOUR OF CECELIA AHERN'S
Mrs Whippy, a play about a middle-aged woman dealing with
life's difficulties and an ice cream addiction. I don't know why
they picked me for the part! Around the same time, I adopted
three very elderly donkeys.

I am a donkey lover, and these were the most adorable
creatures ever, and I fell hopelessly in love with them. Two of
them were snow white. The oldest, Daisy, was a formidable
animal, almost 40 and prone to taking lumps out of me
if I wasn't vigilant. Tarquin was brown and a sprightly 26.
Snowball, the other white donkey, was the sweetest little four-
legged creature I had ever come across: a modest, gentle little
fellow who enjoyed nothing more than getting a great hug.

Two nights before I was to start the Irish tour of *Mrs
Whippy*, the weather changed and the temperature dropped
to minus five. I got up early, expecting to see six pairs of ears
peeping out of the donkey shed. There were only four.

At first I couldn't find Snowball anywhere. Then I spotted

him standing in a corner of the paddock, frozen stiff. He must have left the shed and fallen asleep outside. I tried to get him into the shed, but he tripped in the doorway and fell.

The vet tried everything to save him, but it was too late. I put his head on my lap and said my Buddhist chant for him as he took his last breath. Anyone who loves animals will know what my grief was like. I was distraught.

The next day I headed for Castlebar and the first night of the play. I thought I was over the worst of losing Snowball. I am a farmer after all: my trade depends on livestock becoming deadstock. But the donkeys were different, and I was, in a word, bereaved.

The show went fine, but as the tour progressed, I became more and more down. Now, for one who is normally such a blabbermouth when it comes to depression, I kept my feelings to myself – you can't go round crying your heart out and then telling sympathisers your tears are over a donkey.

That uninvited visitor – inappropriate sadness – was rifling through my house again. I was genuinely very sad

'If you don't know how to die, don't worry;
nature will tell you what to do on the spot,
fully and adequately.
She will do this job perfectly for you;
don't bother your head about it.'
Montaigne, *Essays*

about Snowball, but this sorrow was all pervasive and out of proportion.

When the tour came to an end, it was lambing season at the farm, so I immersed myself in that. I distracted myself with more work, which I am always apt to do.

Looking back on my sorrow at that time, I realise that Snowball's death had something to teach me. I learned to have the courage to be with another being when they are dying. I learned how important the moment of passing is.

Faith in Life

DURING MY STRUGGLES WITH DEPRESSION, AS I'VE TOUCHED upon previously, I have thankfully never felt bad enough to want to kill myself. I have the kind of depression that rarely grinds my daily life to a halt. Routines are observed and I keep going. Despite the internal pain and distress I may feel, my depression isn't as crippling as others'.

Despite never having the urge to take this most decisive step for the depression sufferer – to end it all – it is my understanding that when people take their own lives, or make an attempt to, it's not so much that they want their lives to end as that they want the *pain* to end. I have known people suffering from chronic depression for whom the pain has never abated. Who knows the reasons why – psychological, chemical or otherwise? But I know that in understanding depression, it is down to the sufferer to make a concerted effort to look at the reasons why they are the way they are. The quest to live your best life with depression can be an elusive one, and in many ways it is a quest for faith: faith that there is light in the dark, that life with depression can have its times of joy, of success, of self-realisation, of love, of breakthrough and of moving on, however it manifests. But without inspecting our deeper selves, we can never begin to open ourselves up to this miracle of faith. I'm not talking about religious faith, simply faith in life – a reason to keep going. Self-investigation is about finding out what makes you tick – and that can hold the key to self-acceptance, acceptance of your condition and the peace, uneasy as it may be, that comes with that significant step.

The rising rate of suicide among young people, especially young men, is something we have to respond to on a society-wide basis. Part of the issue, aside from the unprecedented pressures of living felt by today's young people, is that our understanding of the transient nature of difficulties – the ebb and flow of life – develops with age. When we are young, a situation that in time will resolve itself can seem utterly without hope of a resolution. Buddhism has a youth division that emphasises the need for optimism and self-determination – and it really gets results – but these attributes exist outside of any religion and it is essential that young people develop a sense of both these things in order to take ownership of their place in the world, a place with a secure future. The blanket entertainment from screens of one variety or another can act as blinkers both from the pressures of the world but also from taking up your rightful place in it – in an optimistic and self-determined way.

The hyper-sensitivity that comes with depression means that a young person prone to the condition will pick up every shift in dynamic, every little word that might be construed as a put-down, and turn it in on him/herself. Such young people have no outlet for the pain they feel, and no understanding of it. They can think that they are the only ones who feel this way, and that it will never end. They can see taking their own lives as the only way out.

How do we make people feel precious and worthy from the very beginning?

Whereas previous generations of Irish people were taught not to praise their children in case they might get 'big heads', today, we're the opposite. And of course that's a good thing – children need a sense of their own value reflected back at them from the moment they are born. But they also need clear boundaries. It's fine to tell a child that he or she is the best, most wonderful, uniquely fantastic human being since the dawn of

'Any day is a good day to die,
but no day is a good day to take your own life.'
Anonymous teenager,
after recovering from a suicide attempt

sliced bread. But that, in itself, is not necessarily a recipe for adult happiness or self-fulfilment. Rather than indulgence, children need strong love and clear boundaries. And strong love is more about action than words, i.e. it involves a lot of effort, negotiating the boundaries of the world with a child, and leading by example. Also, recognising that the word 'no' is not a bad thing to have in our vocabulary with children. No one is served long term by ongoing instant gratification, despite a consumer-driven world that may go to great lengths to convince us otherwise. Least of all children.

But the truth is that no amount of good parenting, schooling, friendships or otherwise can ensure that a young person will not come into contact with depression. Youth is a time of great upheaval regardless of circumstances, and it's inevitable that some young adults will fall foul of it.

And suicide can be a tragic consequence of this. Families who are left behind face grief of the most extreme kind. As a society we have a duty to them – the same duty that we have to all sufferers of mental health issues – and that is to lift the blanket of shame that remains to this day and become more open about the realities of these issues at every level of society. We need to speak about it like it's a normal part of life – because, sometimes all too tragically, it *is* a normal part of life.

For many of us, it is much easier to have a chat about the latest YouTube clip or talk about a football match than say, 'I am feeling bloody awful and I don't know what to do.'

'And when you die, have everything buried with you.
If the next wife wants it, make her dig.'
Joan Rivers

Through years of work, I have rid myself of the shame I felt about my depression or the symptoms that come with it. If I am getting anxious in a situation, I will tell the person I am with that I am anxious. If I need to leave, I will explain why. And, perhaps because I don't have a problem being open about it, I find that reflected back at me every time. In fact, people really appreciate the honesty, and often it opens the door to a deeper friendship and understanding for both parties.

When it comes down to the bottom line, no one's going to help you until you help yourself.

Goodbye, Mick

I DON'T RECALL MY LAST SCENE IN *GLENROE* WITH MY FRIEND Mick Lally. I have a vague notion that there was a bit of animosity between Biddy and Miley and they weren't really talking at the time of her death. She had turned a significant emotional corner in her life and was driving home, ready to make a new start on her marriage when she had her fatal car crash. There hadn't been many shared scenes before that.

When the cast did the read-through for the episode of

Biddy's death, there was utter silence on the set. I could feel the sadness of my colleagues, could see the big, round eyes looking at me, and I was very touched because I knew they were going to miss me. After work, we all went out for celebration drinks – it was like our own little wake for Biddy. Lord rest her.

Of course, after *Glenroe*, Mick and I would work together many times on stage and to many people's minds we remained Biddy and Miley, a married couple treading the boards. We were starring together in a new production of John B. Keane's *The Matchmaker* when he passed away on 31 August last year, after a long battle with emphysema. Mick was only 64.

During the play's run, he was on top form on the set, and for the most part his breathing was quite good. The run came to its end and, as we parted, he said, 'See you in Dundrum in the autumn,' referring to the play's next run. For a nano-second I thought, 'No, I won't be seeing you,' but then the thought went out of my head.

I didn't see this thought as odd. I suppose, with Mick's illness, it had crossed my mind that the time might come when stage work would become impossible for him. But at no time did I imagine he would die. It came as a huge shock.

Mick was a family man above all else, and he loved the bones of his wife, Peige, and his children Saileog, Darach and Maghnus. They've lost a wonderful husband and father and I can only sympathise with them in their grief.

With Mick's passing, I lost a very good friend, somebody

who was part of most of my adult life and somebody I will miss for ever.

After he died, I got a letter from a farmer who said, 'When I heard he died, I stopped the tractor and pulled over and cried my eyes out.' I think there was something about that era of *Glenroe* that was very comforting for people. I don't think RTÉ realised the sort of iconic status it had and how huge Miley was to the ordinary people of Ireland.

Mick was so recognisable that wherever he went hapless men (who often looked like Miley) would come up to him, thinking he was the harmless gobshite he portrayed on television. They'd get a shock, though. Mick was a force to be reckoned with and they'd often be sent off with a flea in their ear.

The day he died I was asked to go on the *Six One News* and to do several other television and radio interviews and, in Mick's memory, I wanted to oblige. I drove up to Dublin and, when I arrived in the RTÉ campus, expected the usual endless search for a parking space. But that day the nearest parking space to the studio was free.

I went in and did my best, although in my shocked state, it was really difficult to look at all the footage and pictures of Mick and talk about him without breaking down. In between interviews, in an effort to help myself stay calm, I decided to drive out to Seapoint for a swim. If RTÉ is normally bad for parking, Seapoint is ten times worse, but when I arrived, again a parking space right beside the beach was free. I was getting out of the car to go and pay the parking fee when a woman came up and said, 'I'm just leaving and there's time left on my ticket. Would you like it?' So I got free parking.

After my swim, I ended up having a very deep conversation with a lady who recognised me and knew that I had lost a friend. She had a husband who was ill and we empathised with each other. Later that day, after the last interview was finished, I went to collect some drawings that I had left in to be framed as presents for friends. I discovered that I was the ten thousandth customer and so got them for free.

The day of Mick's death was a day of grace.

The next evening, when I went to the wake and saw him in the coffin, I smiled because he was so resolute-looking, in the face of death. He was that kind of man: no matter what he came up against, he just got on with it.

Mick Lally was a great man who helped change the face of Irish theatre as a co-founder of Galway's Druid Theatre Company and he was beloved not only to his family and friends, and all of us in *Glenroe*, but to the people of Ireland. He was a man who had the courage to be himself – uncompromisingly

'I like living. I have sometimes been wildly,
despairingly, acutely miserable, wracked with sorrow,
but through it all, I still know quite certainly
that just to be alive is a grand thing.'
Agatha Christie

truthful and undefended. He told it like it was and he didn't bear grudges.

On the day of his funeral, I made a promise to him to drop resentment from my life. It won't happen overnight. It will require vigilance, but I'm determined to do it.

The Only Certainty

SOMETIMES IN MY MORE FLOWERY MOMENTS, I THINK, 'WOULDN'T it be lovely to see death as the crowning glory of our lives, rather than something to be feared?' It is the only certainty and it still always astounds me that we're all so surprised by it when it happens.

When you live among nature, you see the cyclical nature of life. All things die, rot away and are transformed. Nothing ever truly ends.

I think if we were complete in our humanity, then we would not need to invent eternity for ourselves. I do not believe in heaven, but I certainly believe that life goes on beyond death.

A lot of Buddhists I know would say, 'You've got life *now*. *This* is the living, manifest part of your life. Don't be constantly worrying about death because it is not here. Live while you are alive.'

The Buddhist belief is that when you die, you go into a

thing called Ku, which is like being asleep. The prayers of your predecessors or your people who are still alive buoy you along. And then when the time is right, you manifest again.

If anyone dies who is connected to someone I know, or from around the area where I live, I put them in my prayers. I chant to help buoy them along towards their new manifestation.

Like most human beings, I am afraid of dying, but I don't think about my own death that much. I worry about other people's deaths, about their absence and the suffering that comes with grief.

For myself, I believe that if you can look death in the face, then you can live more fully. I didn't know until after my father had died that he had told the parish priest he knew he was going to die, and he was perfectly happy to go. And I think my mother went in exactly the right way for her.

Buddhism is essentially an atheistic religion, in the sense that there is no greater power. As such, the word 'God' isn't used. But, for me, God is a useful concept, and one which we can readily understand, so I will use the word here, for the want of a better one. Everything is God. You are God. I am God. We are the actualisation of God.

I love coming in at night from my gate and seeing all my neighbours' lights on. To know the belonging, the sense of being rooted, it's something complete. That is God. That is everything. And it is simple.

Living out of the shadow of death is all about letting go. When my time eventually comes, I would like a part of me to remain in Delvin, alongside the spirits of my parents. I would like part of me to be wherever my musician is going to be and I would like part of me to be at Serge Gainsbourg's grave in Montparnasse, Paris. I suppose the only solution, bar chopping me up into three pieces, is cremation, even though the idea of being reduced to ashes doesn't exactly sit easily with me!

Once somebody asked me how I would like to be remembered. Of course, there is part of me that would like to be remembered as a terribly thin and beautiful actress, but beyond being able to turn back time and alter reality, I know I can let go of that one. In truth, though, the only important reviews will be from the people who live in my area. If they say I was a good neighbour, that'll be good enough for me.

10

Home

*'Home is a place you grow up wanting to leave,
and grow old wanting to get back to.'*
John Ed Pearce

The Dance

WHEN I LEFT HOME IN MY TWENTIES TO FIND MY OWN SPACE IN the world, free from the conservatism of country life, I was running blindly with no real intention of ever moving back. But now I realise that I was always on a journey back here: it was always in my lifeblood.

What I've found since moving back is that rural Ireland has changed into a more open, outward-looking place. I've changed too. I am now wise enough to see the value of its traditions and the strength of character of its people. So in a way, through coming home, I've come full circle. It's had a very positive effect on all aspects of my life, from my health to my friendships, to my sense of self and the way I deal with my depression. Coming home has literally earthed me.

One of the more recent plays I was in was *Dancing at the Ballroom of Romance*. Written by my good friend and frequent director Michael Scott, it was staged in the original Ballroom of Romance in Glenfarne, County Leitrim, in the summer of 2009.

The people of Glenfarne and the surrounding areas made up most of the cast, with five professional actors playing some of the principle roles. Michael had devised the script using stories from the fifties and sixties, along with sayings indigenous to that part of Ireland, and the show was an actual night at the dance hall, with the play threading through it. The audience were encouraged to participate by coming dressed in the fashions of the time.

Throughout the play's run, the weather was balmy and I have happy memories of long afternoons sitting in the sun, chatting with the cast and generally larking around. There was so much laughter. Hilarious breakfasts in the guesthouse where we pros, bleary-eyed from the night before, would argue, banter and share anecdotes until we were thrown out because it was time for lunch. After rehearsals, in the little pub across the road from the guesthouse, I would sit chattering with the cast, drinking wine from little cut-glass goblets.

The day of our opening night was like no other in my career. Usually, I'm terrified and spend the day lying low and trying not to panic. But this time I felt altogether more relaxed and that afternoon myself and fellow cast member and friend Sharon O'Doherty went swimming in the local lake. It was idyllic. In between swims while letting the sun dry us off, we marvelled at how calm we were.

The nature of the show meant it was unpredictable, so all we could do was leave our egos at the door and let it happen. So we swam and laughed and embraced life just as it was, before heading off to get into our costumes and make-up.

Ballroom was a great success. It wasn't just a show; it was an event. It was a true community of people of all backgrounds coming together to create something joyful – and it was a joy to work on. The mixture of age groups involved was illuminating, showing that there is really very little difference between the young and the old. There were delightful giggling girls, giddy young fellas, wise and humorous older people, and a few hilarious old codgers who did exactly as they pleased most of the time, director or no director. There wasn't the hint of an 'us and them' feeling between the professional actors and the locals involved. It was just one great big 'us'.

Towards the end of the show each night, an older couple did a solo dance together. This was to symbolise the harmony of a long, loving marriage. Members of the cast filled the sides of the hall to watch and every single time, the dance moved us to tears. If there was ever an example of the grace, elegance and beauty of age, it was that dance. The dancers didn't have to do acrobatics to mesmerise; it was all there in the wisdom of their bodies.

Another aspect of *Ballroom* that was very satisfying for me was that it took place in a largely farming community. I could be discussing the motivation for a line with a cast member one minute, the next we would be bemoaning the 'shockin' low price of wool'. The actor and the farmer were happy bedfellows in Glenfarne that summer. Both aspects of me, which had for so long vied with each other for prominence, now sat comfortably together. It was its own sort of homecoming.

Mind you, back in Delvin, if I'd got an Oscar on Thursday and I sold some cattle Friday, they would be more interested in the price I got for the cattle!

I love where I live. I love being in a community of old farming families that go back generations. I thrive on being part of nature and the rhythms of the earth here. There is, however, one drawback.

Having played a farmer for so many of my acting years, I got into the habit – to try and clearly separate my identity from that of Biddy – of denying my rural roots when I wasn't on the *Glenroe* set. Back then, I was the quintessential urban girl, a far cry from Biddy in her overalls and wellies. In many ways, I'm still that urban girl. I crave the anonymity of the city – that feeling of being surrounded by people but still having privacy. The country has changed and evolved in many ways since I was young, but it still doesn't have the edge you get in the city. I have to go to Dublin once or twice a week and to Paris whenever I can. I need the energy it brings.

As crazy as this might sound, when I visited Japan with my Buddhist group back in the nineties, I thought the Japanese were quite like rural Irish people. They live in a very structured society and have a certain way of saying one thing while meaning another. A person you are talking to will know that you mean something other to your words, and his reply will be something he knows you want to hear.

In rural Ireland, someone could stop you in the street and chat to you for half an hour. Then, just as you're about to say goodbye and go off about your business, she will say, 'Oh, and by the way . . .' and then she'll come out with what she stopped you to talk to you about in the first place.

In its own particular way, rural society is a very sophisticated one, but then all you have to do is walk into the village wearing a hat that might be all the rage in Paris and suddenly you're the talk of the town.

Once I went into the local shop wearing a bandeau-style hat.

'What's that yoke you have on your head?' says the shopkeeper.

'It's a bandeau,' says I. 'I got it in Paris.'

'Well, it's horrible quare lookin',' says he.

After that I returned to standard farmer's issue.

When I moved back home, I continued to find it difficult to manage the two parts of myself – the urban and the rural – and found myself doing far too much to keep them balanced.

I remember one Monday morning during a particularly frenetic tour with *The Field*, I got up very early to count the sheep before leaving home. During my count, I found a lamb flailing about in the river. I had to sort of abseil down a steep bank in the rain and haul the lamb out (thankfully, alive and literally kicking, the little shit). Once that was done, I threw my wet, muddy self into the shower before driving all the way to Skibbereen to for the play. I did it because it had to be done. I had to earn my living.

HOW THE LIGHT GETS IN

'He is happiest, be he king or peasant,
who finds peace in his home.'
Goethe

During that tour, I was doing okay without medication. I wasn't a barrel of laughs but the sadness and unease were at pretty low levels.

If you've ever watched *Star Trek*, you will know that on the USS *Enterprise* there is the constant hum of the engines in the background while the action is taking place. That's a good analogy to describe my day-to-day depression – the unending low hum that underpins everything, but doesn't stop it happening. I can go about the business of daily life, doing my job, whether I'm up to my oxters in muck on the farm or caked in make-up on the stage, but in the background there is a never-ending hum of impending doom. I am going to be punished by some unseen force. For what, I don't have a clue. Maybe just for being myself. Inevitably the hum eventually becomes a roar and I have to do something about it. After that tour of *The Field*, I went back on medication.

Life in the country has become a balancing act as I try to stop the hum becoming a roar. When I go to Dublin or my flat in Paris, I can be myself completely, but in the country, I find I edit myself in order not to alienate people, the way I did when I lived at home in my early twenties. The culchee and the bohemian, headbutting like rams in October.

Running Free

A COUPLE OF YEARS AGO, I DECIDED TO TAKE UP RUNNING IN the hope that it might affect my mood positively. The hum was threatening to become a roar, and although I was walking quite a lot to get the physical outlet I needed, it wasn't cutting it.

So I decided to up the speed a bit. I wasn't satisfied just to buy a pair of good trainers and get out there. No, I had to have the entire kit – shorts, shoes, running T-shirt, headband, goggles – the whole shooting match. You'd think I was Sonia O'Sullivan, but in truth I ran like a sloth in slow motion. Still, the first time I did it, I broke a sweat and my mood improved. After forcing myself out for a few daily 'sprints', the effect was almost miraculous. The hum disappeared.

Anyone who suffers with depression and has learned to manage it will tell you that exercise is key because it is one of the best ways of producing endorphins, those happy little proteins in the body that promote a feeling of well being. On the net, you can find various programmes to get you started. Jeff Galloway (www.jeffgalloway.com) is the online trainer I recommend – he's the one with the least bells and whistles.

As I progressed with my running, I was asked to do the mini-marathon for a local charity, the Westmeath Hospice. Having this goal pushed me even further, but in two directions. On one hand I was getting fitter and fitter, feeling great about myself and my body, on the other I was in an endless competition with myself to run better, faster, longer. I trained assiduously and took myself very seriously as an athlete. I amassed enough running books to stock a library and spent much of my non-practising time studying them, culling enough information to inform an Olympic trainer.

About three weeks before the marathon, my friend Isobel Mahon decided she would enter as well to raise funds for Multiple Sclerosis. She had done no training at all. I clucked disapprovingly to her about possible muscle strain, shin splints, pulled hamstrings and all manner of terrible afflictions 'athletes' like me trained hard to avoid. Isobel took no notice. We arranged to meet before the mini-marathon and run together so I could keep an eye on her, but, in the throng, we missed each other and I ended up running on alone.

After I got to the finishing line, I couldn't find Isobel and couldn't get her on her mobile phone. I pictured her lying in a dehydrated heap somewhere on the course. I rang her landline to alert her partner of the possible crisis. She answered.

Immediately I presumed that sanity had prevailed and she hadn't run after all. 'You didn't make it?' I asked, still out of breath after my exertions.

'I did,' she replied, 'but I had to come home afterwards and have a shower. How did you do?'

The little wagon had run the race, driven to her house in Cabinteely and had a shower while I, the great athlete, was still waddling around the course.

A running tip for depressives: don't turn things into a competition. Setting the bar too high is self-defeating. You run after perfection all the time and berate yourself when you don't achieve it. If you decide to take up running or any form of exercise, take it easy. Trundle along at your own pace and if someone slags you off for your lack of speed, show them two fingers.

For all the books about running I have read, there was only one quotation from an unnamed woman that made me learn anything properly beneficial. She said: 'I realise I have this one speed and I'm not going to get much faster. I just take the attitude that I'll get there when I get there. My outlook is that I'm faster than the people that are watching.'

That's the 'least you can do' philosophy in a nutshell. We'll get there when we get there.

One of the major side benefits of running is that it's changed my relationship with food. From the time I had my brush with anorexia as a teenager, I've been the living definition of the yo-yo dieter, taking the pounds off with the latest fad diet and then putting them back on again the minute I achieved any success.

Food was my drug of choice. If I was having a bad day or in one of my seriously anxious phases, I would eat. There was a time when I could put away toxic amounts of food, the real binge stuff like ice cream, pepperoni pizza, chocolate, chips . . . anything that was fat and carb-laden. Carbs and fat tend to numb the feelings. If I binged on alcohol the

*'I had rather be on my farm than
be emperor of the world.'*
George Washington

way I binged on food, I would have ended up in St John of God's.

Binging on food distracted me from dealing with my depression. It gave me something different to worry about. Instead of trying to deal with the root causes of my depression, I would go on a diet and focus on that. Then the process of getting thinner and putting it back on would begin again.

After I started running, I stopped bothering with the weighing scales. I'm fitter and probably thinner, but I don't really care about my weight the way I did before. The exercise itself gives me the good feeling I used to get from standing on the scales and seeing that I had shed a few pounds.

My urges to binge are few and far between now, but when they do come I will buy a tub of ice cream and eat just some of it. Then I'll feed the rest to the ants, rather than keep it in the fridge where it might get the better of me.

I like what's happened to me with running. The feelings of fitness and well being are second to none, and what's more I am allowing myself to enjoy food as one of life's great pleasures, rather than have a love-hate relationship with it. There's nothing I like better than sitting down to a good meal and really savouring the food.

Friendship

WHILE RUNNING IS A WAY FOR ME TO BEAT THE BLUES, I THINK I would be lost in this life without my friends. The quality of my friendships is very good, and I think I am a good friend too.

Garvan is my best friend. It's a very deep relationship and we have to constantly adjust it to where we are in our lives, learning how to be with each other and properly support each other.

When I am really down, I have friends who are absolutely there for me, like Hazel, who supported me throughout the summer when I was at my lowest ebb, and Isobel, who deserves an ear transplant for all the listening she's done over the years. Most of my friends don't suffer from the kind of chronic depression that I have and sometimes they have to protect themselves from me because I'll be too needy, or frustrated, anxious or cloying. I understand and I don't have a problem with it.

Truth is, we depressives are hard work with a capital *H*.

Despite the boundaries that people have to set up, there is a safe space in a lot of my friendships where I know I can truly be accepted for who I am. But I don't expect to be saved. Good friends can hold you while you are falling, but they can't pull you up. Your friends can't save you, your partner can't save you and, what's more, it's not their mission to save you.

It's taken me a long time to learn this. Once at a Buddhist meeting there was a woman who told everyone that she wished her husband would do a particular thing for her, but he wasn't complying. The moderator told her that her husband was not there to meet her needs. Instead, he was here to relate to her with love and to witness her.

A good friend is a good witness. If I had one piece of advice pertaining to friendship, it would be to listen. We all want to smooth over our friends' problems, give them instant solutions and dry their tears, but that's not what a friend in need really requires.

Simply listen. Even if you want to rush to their aid, just let them keep going. You might have something of help to say after you've really heard and understood what they are going through. Then again, you might not. All that matters is that you are there for them, solidly and in the moment. When your turn comes, they will do the same for you.

My friends and I are similar types. We are all navel gazers. With people who don't navel gaze, even though I might like their company, I quickly lose things to talk about. My friends and I pull things apart, we are dissectors. We are philosophical, we like to investigate existence, the whys and wherefores of life. But we're not adverse to uproarious laughter or ridiculously surreal conversations either.

One good thing to come out of the financial downturn is that people aren't so busy anymore. They have the space to focus on the important things in life, like spending time with friends, escaping from the doom and gloom by simply being silly with their mates. What better fun is there to be had?

These days, I find that I want to go back to my old friends, people I knew years ago that I lost touch with. I would be happy to drive across the country just to have a cup of coffee with some of them.

A few months ago, a bunch of us Glenrovians went to Maureen Toal's eightieth birthday party. It was a panic. Maureen and Eileen Golgan sat in a corner behaving like delinquents, leading us all astray. Emmet Bergin turned up and was his usual charming, outrageous self: the eternal lad. Isobel Mahon, Geraldine Plunkett, Garvan and myself were in the thick of the action, as per usual.

Whenever the *Glenroe* cast get together, I remember what a gift it was to work with them all, and how that for 16 years of my life, with all my ups and downs, some of my happiest times were spent with them. The gift that has lasted is the richness of those friendships.

My Happy Medium

AFTER A FEW YEARS OF LIVING IN THE COUNTRY FULL-TIME, WITH regular trips to Dublin to stay with Garvan, I found that I had stopped going out to socialise. The showbiz me, camp and irreverent, didn't fit in either at home or in the Dublin scene.

In situations where I would meet artists, they seemed cool and worldly, while I felt like a plodding country bumpkin. In the company of country people, I felt like a spare tool, as if I wouldn't be taken seriously because naturally, being from the world of television, I was up myself.

I wasn't at ease anywhere except with animals, and try telling a donkey about your weight worries. And the hens don't give a stuff about the new Tom Murphy play. Over time, I became very lonely – even if I was surrounded by love.

Then, out of the blue, I was asked to appear on RTÉ's *Would You Believe?*, a weekly, half-hour documentary programme about a different person's spiritual life. I was flattered, although I had reservations about showing the viewing public into my real, day-to-day existence. Of course, my inner show-off won the day and I agreed to do the show. Television is my happy medium – I am always drawn to it because I feel very relaxed in front of the camera.

We shot the programme and it was a relaxed and thoroughly enjoyable experience. But the minute the cameras were gone, I started worrying like crazy. For the first time in my life, I had just gone public about myself, my belief system, my partner, my work, even my neighbourhood. When I went into it, I knew what the consequences of doing the programme were, but I didn't really think about them until it was all over.

As luck would have it, I was going to Paris the day before it aired, so I wasn't at home to tune in. On the flight back to Ireland, I steeled myself for the battering that I was sure would come from the media, from my neighbours, from my friends. As it turned out this time, and so many others, my worries were unfounded.

People reacted very well. I received letters, emails, texts and phone calls, all of them supremely positive. Even *The Sunday Times* TV critic liked it!

A strange little fluttering made itself known deep inside. It occurred to me that perhaps part of the reason that I have had such ongoing problems with confidence in my own identity is that for so long my public identity was not my own. It was that of a character I had played for 16 years of my life.

Not long after *Would You Believe?* aired, I was asked to go on *Midday*, the afternoon panel show on TV3 and I jumped at the chance. I always watched the programme and thought the women on the panel were clever, politically astute and very funny. I was looking forward to meeting them.

The first day I walked into the make-up room at the studios, I was shaking with nerves. Fiona Looney and Collette Fitzpatrick were there and when they turned to smile at me, I realised I had thrown myself to the lions, or, in other words, the journalists. I readied myself for questions that I should treat with the utmost suspicion and the certainty that whatever I replied would come out wrong.

As it turned out, all of the women I've met doing *Midday* have been the salt of the earth and the atmosphere on set is, without fail, one of mutual respect. Some of the regular panellists have minds like surgical instruments that can dissect a subject accurately in double-quick time. I tend to see things at very functional level and I'm not great at financial or political analysis, so from the outset on *Midday*, I decided to lean on my humour and common sense in an effort to hold my own.

During that first programme, I was very nervous, but the girls were at my back and kept me going. Like me, they all went through their own first days on *Midday*, so they empathised with me and supported me.

Afterwards, I should have been over the moon. Instead, I found myself wandering around a nearby shopping centre feeling physically ill. I was 100 per cent certain that I had made a total fool of myself, that people would have watched the show and wondered why the hell they had asked me on, I was so bad. My mind went over and over what I had said, wishing I had said everything another way, wanting to go back and erase the whole show so I could do it again, the right way.

Then I got a call from the producer asking me to come back on the following week. They were very happy with my contribution.

My big challenge is having the courage to be who I am and stand on my own two feet. Doing *Midday* has been a huge part of that journey for me. I gather strength from the other women on the show, who come from all walks of public life. There is a great sense of freedom because, for the most part they accept their own vulnerabilities, but aren't afraid to show

'Friends are God's apology for relatives.'
Hugh Kingsmilll

their strengths at the same time. They give me space to do the same.

Since going on *Midday*, I've got more attention than I ever did when I was doing *Glenroe*, and it's very different. People are reacting to Mary McEvoy, not a fictional character called Biddy Byrne. I don't even mind if they react negatively to me because I can be myself fully. What's more, the medium of *Midday* gives me a chance to come back and say what I think.

These days, I'm also an Agony Aunt on Tom Dunne's Newstalk radio show where I get to dispense advice to and interact with lots of people across the country.

For the first time in my life, I feel a sense of the disparate parts of myself coming together. From childhood on, I was neither one thing or the other, a good girl or a bold girl, Calamity Jane or Sabrina, my parent's daughter or my own person, a city girl or a country girl, Biddy Byrne or Mary McEvoy.

Maybe it's that I'm maturing and gaining wisdom, maybe it's the attention I get from being on *Midday*, maybe it's that I'm finally setting myself free from the expectations of others, maybe it's the fact that I was asked to write this book ... maybe it's a combination of all these developments and more, but I finally feel like I am reaching my happy medium. And that's okay for now.

Touching the Void

IN MARCH LAST YEAR, I HURT MY BACK WHILE DOING WARM-UP stretches in the dressing room of the theatre where we were doing *The Matchmaker*. The dressing room was absolutely freezing and, as I stretched, I felt something pull. When I got home that night, I discovered that one of the sheep had given birth to two lambs at the bottom of the yard. It was minus seven degrees, so I had to get the lambs and their mother into the shed to save their lives. As I gathered the lambs in my arms, my back froze and I literally had to crawl, dragging the lambs with me so the sheep would follow me into the shed.

The next morning, I could barely move. Garvan was away, so I phoned my friend Anne McDonnell, who came over immediately. When she arrived, I was standing at the phone in the hall, stiff as a board, having called an emergency doctor to get some help. 'Get a pen and take down this number,' said the unsympathetic receptionist at the other end of the line. 'How the hell can I get a pen?' I cried. 'I can't fucking move!'

Anne sorted out the receptionist and the situation in minutes, getting a doctor out to me in double quick time.

I was left unable to do any work on the farm for several months and had to rely completely on my right hand man John Sheridan, or St John as I call him. I managed to do the play because it was a fairly static role, but lifting or carrying or any kind of hard work was out of the question.

It was lambing season on the farm, which is always a busy and challenging time for anyone involved, not just the sheep. Despite the fact that every fibre in my being was pushing me to exert myself and help with the lambing, because of the pain and stiffness in my legs, I had to give in and become completely inactive at home. On top of all this, I couldn't run, which by now had become my number one, beat-the-blues mechanism.

I finished the run of the show and then tried to surrender to idleness, interspersed with a trip to Dublin now and then to appear on *Midday*. I couldn't do it. I kept trying to do things on the farm, get back to my yoga, clean the house, do anything, but my back refused to heal in line with my schedule, taking its own time instead. I was in quite a bit of discomfort and extremely frustrated.

By May, I had become a basketcase. I was in the midst of the worst bout of depression and anxiety I had experienced in 10 years. I was lurching around with a quaking feeling in my stomach, waking up in the middle of the night with the horrors and suffering from a kind of jittery, all-over restlessness that was hard to bear. For the first time in my life, I wanted to just lie in my bed in a dark room, away from the world, but when I attempted that, the shakes would start and I'd have to get up again.

This depression was so overpowering that there was no running away from it. I had no choice but to take a good look at myself and see what was at the root of it. But first I had to 'up the meds' a bit, to help me get to the point where I was calm enough to self-examine.

Before I'd become completely inactive, I was doing too much for my brain to handle. I was acting, running a farm, trying to fulfil my obligation to publicise the show I was in, doing *Midday*, doing bits and pieces for Newstalk, and driving between Delvin and Dublin nearly every day with a bad back.

I was in constant pain. I had no ability to protect myself from the stress of it all. As I became more bamboozled by the levels of responsibility I had taken on, even trying to be a good girl fell away. I started saying no when I was asked to do new things, but more in an aggressive than assertive way. I was like a very nervous racehorse, kicking out everything that came near in an effort to protect myself.

All my life, I had tried to be all things to all men in order to feel secure, yet, at the same time, I had made big efforts to stand up for myself in the face of what I perceived to be unjust demands or behaviour. In the face of situations that challenged me, I was either hyper-reactive with lots of seething overdramatic 'How dare yous!', or so timid that I became completely ineffective. I couldn't strike a balance between Bambi and a thundering bitch. I had no idea how to protect myself from stressful situations without hurting people's feelings.

Through the process of my self-examination, I learned that the answer was very clear. I had to learn to say no, but to say so, not out of reaction but from a grounded place, where I knew I was doing it for the right reasons, which were for myself.

I began in a very simple way. Anyone who knows me well will tell you that I'm not too keen on visitors dropping in on me unannounced. I like to feel that I can withdraw from company if I'm feeling anxious. If I know someone is coming, at least I can prepare myself and be ready, otherwise I am all at sea, nervous and unable to really be in the moment.

I've been giving myself a hard time about this recently. What kind of person wouldn't be glad to have company? I was just odd and selfish and if people took the hump at my anti-social attitudes, I fully deserved it. Then one afternoon as I was talking to the group of women on the *Midday* set before we went on air, I felt safe enough to voice my misgivings about unexpected visitors. To my great surprise, every one of the women on the panel felt the same way. There I was, isolating myself and self-flagellating over what turns out to be a normal response to the unexpected.

I took stock of my situation and realised that if I didn't have the wherewithal to establish boundaries in an appropriate manner, I would have to keep away from strong-willed people, at least until I gathered my strength again.

It was a strategic retreat of sorts. I also chose to stay away from some of my livelier friends. I was so jittery with nerves and anxiety that the force of their personalities knocked me sideways.

For the first time in the history of my depression, I began to sit with my feelings of sadness and discomfort. It was an internal void that, for so long, I had dreaded tipping over into and being lost within. I would love to say I had a blinding flash of clarity and my depression lifted never to return again. But life is not like that; there are no Eureka! moments.

All I can say is that the void wasn't as frightening as I thought it would be. I was able to immerse myself in it fully. The real life-changing lesson for me during this episode was that I took action based on self-respect. I withdrew a little to give myself space to breathe because I felt I was worth it. My retreat was based in the desire to be myself and accept myself, without the social mask, and to be accepted by others this way too.

Eventually my back healed and I got back to work, both on the farm and on the stage, and my depression lifted. It was the worst bout in years and I never want to go back there again. Yet because of it, I did some work on myself that I think will stand to me greatly in the future. In touching the void, I came into myself.

Epilogue

'Sanity is a cosy lie.'
Susan Sontag

No More Shame

ALL THROUGH THE YEARS WHEN I WAS PLAYING BIDDY, I KEPT MY personal life strictly to myself. My hidden vulnerability was so acute, I was afraid to allow the media to see beyond the façade I had created in case I broke down altogether. I first went public about suffering from depression through an unusual set of circumstances.

It was about nine years ago, and I found myself in a pub, chatting with a journalist about, of all things, the bizarre messages people left on answering machines. I had been on the receiving end of prank calls from an unidentified number, and an anonymous man was leaving messages of, shall we say, an unwelcome nature. As I recounted the story, the journalist asked if they could have it for the following Monday's newspaper.

Mum was still alive at the time and I knew she would be mortified to read about it, so I asked him not to. The journalist kindly asked if I had anything else for him, so I shared the fact that I suffer with depression. As stories go, it was far less salacious.

Sure enough, the following Monday, a story appeared based on our conversation. I'd been long enough in the business to understand how newspapers worked, one story leading to another on the same theme, and then another, but I still didn't put two and two together until I got a call from a different journalist a few weeks later. He was doing a story about depression.

Mary McEvoy, to date filed under *B* for Biddy, was now filed under *D* for depression.

Despite the fact that it was something deeply personal to me, I found that I was actually more comfortable with this type of publicity: after all, it reflected truly, for once, part of who I actually was. People began to write or come up to me on the street and thank me for being so open about something that was so hidden. Sufferers of depression told me that hearing me talk about the condition helped them. In nearly every case, the person confiding in me felt isolated and unable to talk to anyone in their family or circle of friends about their difficulties. They said I was brave.

This fired me up, because I don't think you should need to be brave to talk about mental health problems. I think that discourse about depression should be commonplace. Depression is not a shameful thing. It's not weird. The sufferers are not 'mad'. If there is to be any greater understanding of depression, we need to talk about it openly and unashamedly.

I have a theory about the shame associated with depression and other mental health issues. I believe that people suffering from mental health difficulties hold up a frightening and inconvenient mirror to society. I don't think there's a person alive who hasn't teetered on the brink of the abyss. Those of us who have actually fallen in are an uncomfortable reminder that the flipside of a shiny-happy life is just a tripwire away. So we turn away from the mirror, and, in turning away, we don't allow ourselves to accept fully the reality that depression is a part of life.

The worst thing someone can say to a depressed person is 'pull yourself together'. Years ago, before I realised I suffered from depression, when I'd hear this, I'd go away believing I was just a weakling, while there were people in the world who were far worse off than me, people who had real problems.

Depression is both a psychological and physiological condition. In many cases, the depressed person can neither grasp the idea of pulling themselves together nor physically do it. Telling us to pull ourselves together denigrates depression to a bad mood that anyone can easily cast off instead of recognising it as a real, and often insurmountable, mental health condition. The 'pull yourself together' attitude adds to the silence and shame around depression by pretending it doesn't exist.

Similarly, depressed people who need to take medication should not be ashamed of taking the chemical route. Nobody says don't take your insulin if you are diabetic. Nobody says don't take painkillers if you are in chronic pain, or aspirin to thin your blood if you have a heart condition.

Since the menopause, I have taken medication fairly consistently. It's helping me deal with a chronic illness and I've been outspoken about the fact that I take it. I'm sometimes approached by people who tell me I'm taking the lazy route out, rather than doing something to tackle my depression that requires effort.

I can't say how much this attitude upsets me. I'm upset for myself, of course, but more so for the many people who are taking similar medication who aren't so open about it, who feel ashamed because they're being told they are lazy.

There is no laziness in making proactive decisions to take care of your mental health. Medication may be a last resort for many, and I wouldn't necessarily ever advocate it as a first resort, but if it helps, it should be accepted rather than feared.

Moving Beyond Fear

ONE THING I'VE LEARNED THROUGH MY DEPRESSION IS THAT there's no point in trying to predict the future. Many of the terrible things I feared while in the depths of my anxiety never came to pass. One of my greatest worries for a long time was how I would cope when my parents died, but when they did eventually pass over, while the grief was terrible, it didn't kill me. In fact, my grief over my father's death brought me to a point where I could name my depression and do something about it and, since my mother has passed on, I have come very much to terms with our relationship and feel closer to her than ever.

Fear of an unknown future is a major factor for people right now. Many who suffer from depression and many who don't have grave fears about their financial future. But I think the current recession is a huge opportunity to change our expectations, to turn away from fear and find some happiness.

Every generation wants the next generation to have more, to have better lives and not to suffer as much. But during the boom, I think young people suffered more through getting more. For many parents I came into contact with, life had become more about giving *things* to their children than giving them what they really needed: *time*.

The Celtic Tiger was like a hypnotist. So many of us fell under its spell and wanted more, more, more. We couldn't get enough.

Now, when I listen to the radio or read newspapers, I think we're being hypnotised to believe the opposite – that we have nothing and deserve nothing. Fear is being created and we are acting out of that fear. It's self-perpetuating, and I believe it doesn't correspond to reality.

We need to move on from the shock of the boom ending and take stock of what we actually do have. But our journey towards understanding the true nature of our wealth – as opposed to our assets – has to be cohesive. It has to be about working together.

I'm not talking about forming bloody political parties or pressure groups or any of that lark, but we should be working towards valuing life in small ways, with our neighbours, within our communities.

A few months ago when I was on *Midday*, a woman called in. She was 58, articulate and well educated. She had lost her job and didn't know what was going to happen to her. That day, she had put her hand in her pocket and found a fiver, so it was a good day, but generally her days were long, empty and full of fear.

None of us knew what to say to her: in fact anything we said would have sounded like a platitude. But her call haunted me for days afterwards. I was really trying to figure out what would be of value to say to people who find themselves in a similar position.

I came to the conclusion that everyone has something to offer at this time of hardship. If that woman sat down and made a list of her skills and abilities, even if it's only making a good pot of tea, she could then offer those skills to a voluntary organisation and thereby create value in society, for herself and others.

'The most terrifying thing is
to accept oneself completely.'
Carl Jung

Epilogue

Doing something proactive is far better than sitting with your head in your hands, worrying about what may happen in the future. Plus, you never know what's going to come back to you from what you give out. As long as you're giving out something. Doing something.

Recently, I called round to my neighbour's house. We had a lovely chat sitting beside the range with a cup of tea – and it set me up for the evening. Another neighbour arranged to call up to me soon after that. She brought a pile of magazines and we sat together quietly flicking through them and knitting. I enjoyed it far more than if I had gone out to dinner with George Clooney. Well, okay, marginally more, but more nonetheless! I felt wealthy in that moment, because I was experiencing something truly valuable: quiet harmony with another human being.

We have to create happiness together, starting in small units. It has to be how we act as neighbours, how we treat each other every day in our communities. Not through big, extravagant gestures, but through small acts of kindness. The small things you do are like bricks. Wonders of the world like the Taj Mahal were built with bricks.

I fully admit that it takes somebody who is superhuman or super-rich not to worry about money, and sometimes I wrestle with my own financial fears. But with the 'least you can do' philosophy, you act in the now, not out of the fear of tomorrow, so I change the fear by doing something positive for myself.

Moments of Transcendence

A BOOK ABOUT DEPRESSION CAN'T HAVE A TRADITIONAL HAPPY-ever-after ending. For people who suffer from the condition as I do, there will be no blinding flash of clarity where we leave all our sadness behind and skip carefree into the sunset.

In my years of trying to find my own happy ever after, I have seen many alternative practitioners who told me they could cure me by giving me the right supplements, or by laying hands on me, or by giving me the right affirmation to use in my daily life. I have seen counsellors and therapists who have helped me look at my formative years in a different way. All of these experiences have helped in different ways. But nothing has cured me.

I have come to the conclusion that there is no such thing as a cure. You live with the condition and the best you can do is to find a way to manage it. Combined with medication, the 'least you can do' regime works for me, but only if I continue to be vigilant, gauging my moods and respecting myself enough to protect myself at times of stress.

My spirituality helps me. Chanting in front of my altar each morning and evening bookends my day, giving my life a much-needed structure. In between, I look for moments of transcendence, a connection to the greater universe of which I am one tiny, intricate part.

One blustery, autumnal day many years ago, I was in a field counting cattle. Out of the blue, I was overwhelmed by a sense of the oneness of everything. It was as if, in that moment, I experienced the immensity of time and space and the perfection of the universe. It was an extraordinary feeling and at once it seemed absurd to be unhappy or worried about anything, because everything was a part of an immense and elegant pattern.

Of course, the feeling didn't last – it was so overpowering, it couldn't possibly have – but it came unbidden and it was sublime.

Since then, I have come to value ordinary moments of transcendence in my life because they lift me out of myself and away from the depression that's always there.

My ordinary moments of transcendence come when I dive into the sea or a lake and feel the natural water envelop me.

When I'm sitting beside my partner in silence and realising how perfect it is.

When I'm in the throes of raucous laughter with my friends.

In that moment, when I go outside and *feel* the turning of a season.

When I look at my neighbours' houses and realise that I don't want to live anywhere else, and how much I care for all of them.

The Advantages of Depression

WE ALL WANT TO AVOID DIFFICULTIES. IT'S NATURAL TO WANT everything in the garden to be rosy, but every garden has slugs, bugs, nettles and all manner of things we deem to be undesirable. The ordinary magic of life, however, is that everything – even misfortune – has a function.

I believe the important thing is not to sleep walk through life, not to be so intent on avoiding the challenging things that you choose not to explore the gift of your existence. When I say gift, I don't know who or what the hell gave it to us, but we have it nonetheless. We have life.

Through exploring my condition, I have found several advantages in it. As I've touched upon, having precious little self-esteem lowers the bar of expectancy so much that the only way is up. I think that is why I have come to appreciate what is perceived as ordinary so much. On that evening in Paris when my medication kicked in for the first time, I was so delighted at just being able to enjoy myself and be with people without anxiety, that I forgot about asking for the moon when I could have the stars.

I don't ask for the moon anymore. Not because I think I don't deserve it. It's just that the ordinary things I see and experience around me have become enough. I think that's a far easier adjustment for someone like me to make, easier than for someone who feels an unquestioning sense of entitlement.

Epilogue

When you labour under the illusion that you are driving the bus that is your life, it is twice as hard to learn the lessons misfortune can offer.

So, life goes on. I challenge myself. I feel bad; I get over it and move on. With each challenge, I win a little in the battle for self-acceptance.

I still want to be able to rest properly, to have peace of mind. But I am learning to live with the exasperation of not having that. I still struggle to think well of myself or the work I do, but I can live with that too.

I continue to want to go forward in my acting career. When you have been in the limelight, however accidentally, it is hard to fade into the background. If you have been well known, it is necessary to keep working to stay visible. So I still continue to be a notice box who doesn't really feel at ease with notice, which may seem like a contradiction in terms to you, but it's perfectly normal to me. As they say in my neck of the woods, I'm a quare oul' thing. But it takes all sorts. I'm going to keep on trying to be the best quare oul' thing I can.

'Live like a mud fish,
whose stain is bright and silvery,
even though it dwells in the mud.'
Ramakrishna

Let Go

THE SURPRISE OF WRITING THIS BOOK HAS BEEN THAT IT HAS completed a circle with my parents. At the beginning, I worried that in writing about them that I would let them down, because I would be talking about their relationships with me in public. But, more than anything, I feel this book is an expression of my love for them and my great appreciation of them.

Now they have gone, I believe that even though they are no longer my living parents, and even though they have their own missions in the eternity of life, our connection is so strong that I believe we will meet again in another life.

Mysticism and madness have always been viewed as uncomfortably close to one another and I can just about hear the men in white coats coming to take me away, but whether it's madness or mysticism, I have faith that life is multi-layered and that the past, present and future loop around one another in ways that, so far, we have no explanation for. This faith comforts me.

Of course, I have moments of doubt. We all lose faith at times in our life – that's the nature of humanity. If we accept that about ourselves, we can return to faith with more ease. Quite a lot of the time, my condition causes me to say to myself: 'What's the use?' At times like that, I tell myself that, just as it seems like it's pointless to carry on in faith, it is

Epilogue

'Only one feat is possible —
not to have run away.'
Dag Hammarskjöld

equally pointless to stop having faith. I chant and I trust. I chant and I don't trust. I keep on chanting.

I'm playing for time. Things always improve: that's the truth about being alive, whether you have faith or not. Life is not static. It's a constantly moving spiral and it will always surprise you. Just be prepared to wait. Be modest. Know that no one promised you an easy ride.

If in the dark times you can say to yourself, 'Yes, this is an awful time in my life, but it will get better', then that's a beginning. After that, release your desire to set a timetable for when it gets better. Understand that life has its own timetable and, more often than not, it won't tally with yours. So just let go. It's as simple as that.

I wrote this book because there is a part of me that thinks I might have something of value to say.

The minute I wrote that sentence, I thought: Who the hell do you think you are, Mary? But I believe that everybody has something of valuable to impart. Every person in this universe has something of value, is something of value. We're not all lucky enough to get books published, I know, but we all have something we can share with the world, however small.

I hope I can pass on something to share. If someone who is thinking of taking their life could read this book and think about the little things they can do to make life work in their favour, that would be amazing.

Through examining my depression without shame, I want people to realise that there is no shame in depression. There is always a tomorrow. There is always something new to happen. There is a crack in everything, and the light will always get in.

Epilogue

Have patience with everything unresolved in your heart
and try to love the questions themselves,
as if they were locked rooms or books
written in a very foreign language.
Don't search for the answers,
which could not be given to you now,
because you would not be able to live them.

And the point is to live everything.
Live the questions now.
Perhaps then, some day far in the future,
you will gradually, without even noticing it,
live your way into the answer.

Rainer Maria Rilke

Acknowledgements

Heartfelt thanks to Brian Finnegan and my editor Ciara Considine for the 'steerage'.

To all the people of Delvin and Ballyhealy.

To everyone mentioned by name in the book.

To my relations, the Caseys, the Doyles (especially Mary Doyle RIP), the Killians, the Maloneys and the Morgans.

Rosaleen Cullen, Gillian Powell, Mary Hereward RIP.

To the Parisian gang, Kathleen Cass, Jody Traynor RIP, Monique Becker and Helena Bercau.

The thespian gang, Caroline Fitzgerald, for the work. Ronan Wilmot, ditto. Brian MacLochlainn, ditto ditto.

I apologise if I've left anyone out, but you know who you are, and I thank you.